How To Survive Sales

Contents

Introduction 4
Chapter # 1 5
   Clearing up some Misconceptions 5
Chapter # 2 12
   Why can Anyone Sell 12
Chapter # 3 15
   What makes you Unique 15
Chapter # 4 18
   Why Sales, why Now? 18
Chapter # 5 23
   Where to Start 23
Chapter # 6 32
   The First 90 Days 32
Chapter # 7 41
   Pitfalls and How to Avoid Them 41
   To be distracted 41
   Don't take notes 43
   Do not keep in touch with former clients 46
   We are not planning the day effectively 48
   Don't organize sales tools. 51
   Don't be proud of your work. 52
   They are not keeping up to date 57
   Rushing to sell 59
   Do not use proof of people 62
   Humiliate oneself 64
   Take rejection personally 66

Don't take responsibility 69
Do not show a competitive spirit 71
We are not getting enough information 74
It does not know when to stop talking 77

Chapter # 8 81
20 things you should do (and not do) to make a sale 81

Chapter # 9 87
The 3 "traps" (and more) of salespeople who almost always sell ...87

Chapter # 10 89
The Best Practices for Increasing Sales 89

Chapter # 11 99
How to be good at your job? 99

Chapter # 12 104
The commandments of a good salesperson! 104

Chapter # 13 113
Habits of incredibly successful salespeople 113

Conclusion 123

Introduction

Inside this book, I have discussed strategies from Failure to Success in Selling. This book reveals particular practices and describes the foolproof policies that he displayed and developed. This book gives informative anecdotes and step-by-step guidelines on improving the style, quality, and appearance of a leading seller. No problem what you sell, you will be more productive and effective—and more critical to your business—IF you apply this book rules.

In this volume, we will explain the following contents.

- Clearing up some Misconceptions
- Why can Anyone Sell
- What makes you Unique
- Why Sales, why Now?
- Where to Start
- The First 90 Days
- Pitfalls and How to Avoid Them
- Best Practices and Next Steps
- How to become good at your Job
- And many more...

Chapter # 1

Clearing up some Misconceptions

Misconception # 1: salespeople tell salads

Word mill, huckster, bullshit ... everyone's imagination has the wrong image of the salesperson. "TV shows often relay the image of the nasty salesman who scams and who would be able to sell father and mother," says Nicolas Caron, co-founder of the business management firm Halifax Consulting. If its objective is undoubtedly to sell, it is also responsible for retaining customers; lies would then serve its mission. Lying to sell is a cliché as negotiation techniques become more and more sophisticated.
Another method implemented in sales techniques, behavioralist, requires a strict methodology far from the mistaken idea of spiel. For Nicolas Caron, "knowing how to speak well is not enough; being a salesperson is a demanding job. You also have to be able to deal with failure. You can be good, be in control, and fail to close a sale. You have to constantly question yourself, be able to achieve excellence, to work, to shine...".

Misconception # 2: it is not an evolving profession

Suppose the sales function is accessible from Bac + 2 to Bac + 5. In that case, it is common for recruits to access sales, marketing, or purchasing manager positions after only a few years of experience in a large group. In small businesses, they can be called upon for management positions or key account managers. According to the Director of Corporate Relations at Nonvacua business school, "there are many opportunities for salespeople to grow. He can claim a management position but also be entrusted with increasingly complex negotiations over a larger territory. For the best, missions abroad are also possible. In addition, a phenomenon is emerging and becoming more and more common: today sales managers can become general managers".

To qualify for career development, results, personal investment, and geographic mobility are inherent criteria in the same way as the economic context of the company. "The evolution depends on the size of the company and the opportunities created there. But the main thing is to learn in the field, to accomplish the tasks of his function perfectly and then to think of an evolution", we confide at Nonvacua business school. Without forgetting the possibilities to evolve in an international environment for bilingual salespeople.

Misconception # 3: constantly under pressure

Considered as a nomad, the salesperson goes up and down to carry out his prospecting. But for Arnaud de Saint Quentin, sales representative at Olivier Bertrand Distribution, this is what makes the activity attractive: "what I appreciate in my Job is precise all these trips, the various meetings with customers, the unforeseen to manage. Every day is different. It's very stimulating! ".

Regarding business life, the groups do everything they can to keep their talents and offer their sales representatives activities to make people green with jealousy: sporting meetings, cooking classes, "murder parties" to highlight the spirit of cohesion. Contests are also organized, like the Century 21 "Specialists" challenge, with stays, state-of-the-art gifts...

Misconception # 4: it's poorly paid

The **remuneration** is in two parts, one fixed and the other hand variable. The salary is generally distributed at 75% fixed and 25% variable. The variable portion corresponds to the objectives achieved and the sales made. It can double the salesperson's salary!

According to research carried out by the recruitment firm UPTOO, specializing in sales professions, the salary of sales representatives is much higher than the average French salary. The average salary for a beginner profile is around € 37,700 per year. The Director of Corporate Relations at Nonvacua business school confirms: "once in post, 60% of the school's young graduates earn a total of € 38,000 gross per year".

But education and experience influence pay. Thus, salespeople from **engineering schools** have a salary 34% higher than the national average salary. A confirmed salesperson can earn up to € 65,300 per year. And this, not to mention the benefits in kinds such as the company car and the smartphone.

Misconception # 5: marketing is better

In business schools, the majority of students prioritize marketing. "More intellectual" function, a sort of royal road, according to them. In their eyes, the commercial process is not very rewarding. Yet marketing and sales go hand in hand and cannot exist without each other.

On the other hand, selling requires listening, understanding, and analyzing the customer's needs. "Situational intelligence and rapid adaptability are essential. You have to take the trouble to identify the most appropriate times to meet the client," notes the Director of Corporate Relations at Nonvacua business school. And to add: "the sales sector is one of those which recruit the most, it is one of the most prominent professions in the world. We will always need to sell something, be it products, services, ideas, etc. "—so, convinced?

Common misconception # 6: The salesperson works in the store

At the executive level, sales jobs in stores and distribution networks only represent 15% of job offers for young graduates. 85% are B2B Commercial offers to develop business between companies.

Misconception # 7: Selling is a low recognition and poorly paid profession

As in many trades, there is a wide variety of positions that require sales skills. Ask John Leahy, Airbus Chief Business Engineer, if he finds he receives low recognition and is poorly paid: he will probably tell you that he has increased market share. Airbus from 18% to 50% between 1995 and 2013 by selling 4,948 planes for an amount at the list price of 554.2 billion euros and that he has no problems ...

Misconception # 8: The salesperson is not a manager

The manager's vision responsible for a substantial team is a very limiting vision of the responsibilities and the interest of the positions in a company. The salesperson is often a project manager to bring business to fruition and influence the decision-making of group decision-makers in his company and at his client's premises. The management skills of the people are being developed in an accelerated manner in the sales profession.

Common misconception # 9: The commercial profession is not strategic

You are much more likely to speak to a CEO while working as a B2B salesperson than, for example, while working in a marketing or finance function. Indeed, very often, to sell solutions with high added value, it is necessary to understand the investment priorities of the client companies and, therefore, to speak to the CEO. Talking to a CEO cannot be improvised. It requires a combination of relationship and analytical skills that will pull you to the top.

Misconception # 10: The salesperson only does telephone prospecting

Prospecting is part of the sales cycle. In B2B (sales intended for companies), it is an activity that requires both analyses to succeed in targeting and a vital mastery of communication to be relevant and impactful. A salesperson often does prospect to build up his initial customer portfolio. Then, a balance is established between prospecting time and the loyalty of acquired customers.

Misconception # 11: The salesperson can sell anything to Anyone

The role of the salesperson in B2Bis, first of all, to fully understand the needs and the challenges of his client. It is up to him to identify and target customers who may have a strong need for the solution he offers. Good salespeople will refuse to sell if the customers' needs do not correspond to the proposed solution.

Misconception # 12: The salesperson spends his days negotiating the "fat tip."

Commercial negotiation proper does exist, of course. Typically, it will only represent 10% of a salesperson's time and the skills developed are critical for any manager because, in business, everything is negotiated: business, increases, careers, resources for your projects ...
The ultimate of the sale is to have worked so well upstream in discovering the customer's need that the latter no longer asks himself the question of negotiating the price at the end of the sales cycle.

Misconception # 13: The salesperson goes door-to-door

This type of sales canvassing is limited to certain companies and concerns only B2C sales: to the end consumer. It does not concern B2B salespeople: sales to companies.

Chapter # 2

Why can Anyone Sell

The scientifically proven principles that why Anyone can make sales:

Reciprocity:

It is the obligation to return what you are given. A waiter increases their tip by 3% if they offer a mint candy to a customer. 14% if he gives 2. And 23% if he puts the shapes.

Tip 1: Be the first to donate. Personalize your gift and put the shapes in it.

Rarity:

Anything rare has more value!

When British Airways announced the end of the London / New York Concorde double route, sales exploded.

Tip 2: Emphasize the rarity of what you are offering. The principle of "limited stock" is a hit!

Authority:

If it's an expert who says the product is good, why not believe it. This is how scientists in white coats sell tubes of toothpaste or toothbrushes in advertisements.

Note that if an expert displays his diplomas, his sales become considerable.

Tip 3: Become credible by posting your credentials and recommendations.

Consistency:

If a person agrees to take the first step, there is a good chance that they will continue in this momentum.

Thus, if residents agree to stick a road safety sticker on their car, they will be 400% more committed than those who watch a shocking campaign on TV, for example, and will be ready to follow up with other more impactful actions.

Tip 4: If you get the first move, the game is won. The idea of a sticker is very effective. Who will refuse to support a cause without having to spend money ... at first?

Affinities:

We are more likely to admit offers from our friends or people who look like us (or seem like us).

According to a study conducted on MBA students, the "conversion" rate goes from 55% to 90%.

Tip 5: Find common ground with someone you want to convince. Share them, become an accomplice and... sell your services or your products.

The Consensus:

Humans tend to follow the example of their fellow human beings. So, if we know that 75% of the people who frequented the hotel, we spend the night in reused their towel the next day rather than changed, how do you think we react?

We are 33% more to reuse it too. We follow the social example.

Tip 6: Always have stats to show or show!

Chapter # 3

What makes you Unique

Selling is a challenge as the competition is fierce, and there is no shortage of excellent, well-trained salespeople. Yet before selling a commercial is a human being who meets another human, and therefore other values are at stake.

Unfortunately, this is a commonplace that is far too widespread in people's minds: a salesperson is someone who can sell anything to Anyone and has only one goal: the result. We have all experienced particular situations, faced with a seasoned salesperson who made us buy anything; even though we came up with the idea of purchasing a classic coffee maker, we left with the top model. range and overpriced. As soon as you take the time to reflect for a few minutes on the different techniques to be implemented to be an excellent salesperson, and whatever the product is sold, it is clear that a superb salesperson should not sell! Is a salesperson the one who does not sell? Explanations.

The excellent salesperson is the one who does not sell

Although this sentence seems very surprising, it is evident that the competent, experienced, and professional salesperson is the one who will have the capacity to advise you, to guide your choice without giving the impression of being attracted only by the number and the profit.

That he will withdraw from his sales. Whatever the product sold, whatever the point of purchase studied, it is clear that the best salespeople are those who leave this very particular impression in the minds of customers: "Hey, this salesperson was extremely nice, it shows that he does not do this job to do tricks but to advise above all!". As soon as the client comes out with this idea in mind, it is won, and this is the very proof that this salesperson is the one who advises, who directs, who provides information, who offers but who does not sell.

The human relationship above all

If we come back for a moment to the very basis of the commercial relationship, let us not forget that the human being remains at the center of all commercial activities. Without human relational behaviour adapted to the situation, both the customer and the seller cannot get the most out of this same relationship. This notion is felt in the rise of entrepreneurs like Serge Papen, CEO of Systems U. It was guided by a desire to stay close to his customers and create human-sized supermarkets that he could achieve the success we know.

Some tips for selling better

So, while the sale amount remains the number one goal in a business relationship, it's essential never to put the human side of things aside. Indeed, the salesperson can sell his product or service without giving the impression of it. Still, he is also the one that shows a specific capacity to maintain quality human relations. A word of advice to all salespeople: know how to live up to the expectations of your customers, learn how to show undeniable human qualities, respect, frankness. Another important tip: be yourself and not the caricature of the salesperson you think you are. I prefer to help, inform, accompany than sell, profit, and deceive. In this way, the person in front of you will have increased confidence and will not feel that you are just one customer among many, and you, you will not be a salesperson only capable of selling.

Chapter # 4

Why Sales, why Now?

This is the reason why sales why now.

1- Recruiters tear them away

According to a Manpower study, the shortage of qualified profiles in the trade has never been so glaring for 12 years. Salespeople were the most sought-after profiles between the two lockdowns in 2020.
Whatever the region or even the international desire of the future graduate, there is, therefore, no risk of struggling to find a job as a customer or sales manager.

2- No need for long studies

Unlike jobs just as technical and well paid (in data or cybersecurity, for example), you don't need to study for a long time to become a salesperson.
For example, Open Classrooms' commercial attaché training lasts an average of **six months**. To follow it, no prior training is required, not even the Bac. Following this training, students hold a diploma recognized by the State and have acquired the appropriate skills to find a customer, business, or sales manager position.

3- Attractive salaries, regardless of experience

Since the profession is in tension, commercial profiles are now sought after by employers. The latter contact them regularly to offer them versatile positions with good salaries, including both an often-interesting variable and benefits in kind (mutual, CE, etc.).

For example, the Up To study carried out in 2019 on more than 50,000 salespeople confirms that the average salary of a young graduate in Germany is more than € 34,600 and that the average wage of salespeople in Germany is € 49,700, including € 11,000 of a variable.

In addition, the base salaries of salespeople are matched with a variable team or individual compensation that often provides access to significant settlement in the event of the achievement of objectives.

4- A very versatile function

The Job of a salesperson is fascinating because no day is like another.

Among the missions of professionals in the field, we find a strategy (defining the key messages to sell a product or a service, choosing the brands to canvass, etc.), prospecting, conducting customer meetings, negotiation, customer loyalty, and other various missions.

5- Not sitting on a chair all-day

Being in charge of a client portfolio means, in most cases, that the salesperson visits him. Therefore, the Job of account manager involves travel, and the Job of sector manager all the more. Therefore, if a person wishes to be away from the offices often, they can consequently choose a position with a vital component of meetings or even frequent business trips.

6- Develop valuable human qualities

To excel as a business manager, some behavioral skills are helpful:
- The ability to speak in public to present an offer or a service;
- Empathy and nuanced psychological analysis of his interlocutor;
- The ability to adapt to the other in a discussion;
- Knowing how to work in a team
- Perseverance and patience ...

These qualities are necessary for the field of sales and also in other specialties: customer service, communication, or marketing.

7-... As well as skills sought

A good salesperson knows how to canvass customers, make contact, argue, negotiate, establish and sign a sales contract, retain customers, have excellent interpersonal skills, and the ability to manage several files at the same time while knowing how to prioritize them.
Here too, these skills can be put forward to recruiters.

8- See the impact of his work directly

According to Region Jobs, 90% of bosses believe that the sales function is at the company's heart. Because what could be more precious for them than to canvass, convince and retain their customers?

The results of salespeople directly impact the health of the company, which can be very motivating if you like to know how you are contributing to the company's excellent health daily.

9- Have affluent development prospects

After a few years of experience, the number of clients increases, as do the responsibilities.

The commercial attaché can progress to a position of:
- Business developer / Business development manager
- Account Manager / Key Account Manager
- Specialist in a sector of activity or international
- And then manage a team of salespeople by becoming Manager / Sales Director.

Cross-cutting developments are also possible. Thus, marketing, purchasing, customer service in Spain and abroad are options after starting a career as a business manager.

10 - An entrepreneurial school

Any entrepreneurial project requires defining a sales pitch, prospecting to find customers, convincing them, and retaining them.

Therefore, having experienced the sales cycle in one or more structures is an excellent exercise for those who dream of starting their own business. To the best of my mind!

Chapter # 5

Where to Start

We are not born a "good salesperson." The famous commercial fiber, the innate "thatch" that would allow you to sell anything to anyone, are myths.
Seasoned salespeople sometimes seem like it's easy, but, they've worked really hard to make it happen. Believe me, being a good salesperson can be learned!

Take the time to develop, master, and **perfect your sales techniques.** To repeat his speech, his presentation, his telephone pitch, tirelessly, to know him inside out and have the agility to deviate from it in order to better respond to customers. Anticipate all possible objections and have an answer adapted to each one... These are the real rules for a **good start in sales.**

Whether you're a salesperson at the start of your career or looking to get back to the basics of selling, these tips are essential for success.

If you're new to sales, start with the end: your goals. To get started, you need to know where you are going, have your numbers in mind and measure your performance against them. This is the most important starting point.

When I started my sales career, my managers gave me goals from the first month. A number of appointments per week, a number of new customers per month, and a turnover for the month and the quarter. I have never been so stressed as I was during this period ...

With hindsight, you will see that the stress of objectives becomes positive, that it pushes us to surpass ourselves (if they have been well thought out, of course). In the meantime, ask yourself the right questions to understand them serenely:

- How many clients do you need to achieve your sales?
- What is the average basket of your first sales?
- What are the signature deadlines?
- How many leads/contacts do you need to turn so many leads into customers?
- How many appointments (call/video, physical) do you need to sign a deal and achieve your goals?
-

Define personal goals, ambitions that will motivate you to move forward. It is very easy to recognize the best salespeople in a company. They show leadership, business agility and go all the way. These actions usually precede good results.

Strive for the top three in the organization. It will not happen tomorrow, nor will it be easy, but it always aims at the pursuit of the best in order to reach the top.

Stop improvising

Selling is not an art; it is a science. I know I wrote a book about "The Art of Making Sales", and it's still an art, but bear with me.

If you think of going for talent - as the youngest of us would say - you will go right into the wall.

Some things are fixed in the sale. To get a client to sign, you must understand their issues, identify their shortfalls, generate interest in your product and define a commercial action plan.

Others, on the contrary, are unique and require quick understanding in order to be successful. Every business has its own sales cycle. The way you deal with our clients is unique to your business. If you apply what you have learned without adapting to your industry, you are bound to miss out on opportunities.

Prepare your negotiations to sign more deals.

Before you jump headlong into prospecting, get to know your market. Ask your sales manager or a senior salesperson to train you on products, technical specificities, competitive advantages, classic issues for your prospects, their most frequent objections (price, competition, etc.). Make sure you have a better handle on what and to whom you are selling. In short: get ready!

1. Go back to the client's issues.

You must be able to identify the real issue of your prospect and separate it from the rest of his operational issues.

You don't go to the doctor for a scratch - but when you're nailed to the bottom of your bed ... Asking a salesperson for help is the same thing. The pain must be real. Imagine, if management talks about it every day to find a solution, a budget will necessarily have been allocated to solve the problem. If this is a determining factor for the success of their business, you will have a boulevard ahead of you.

As a salesperson, you need to build trust with your prospects. They need to make sure that you understand them, that you understand their language, their business issues and that you are the right person with the right resources to solve them. In their eyes, you are the expert in the field on which they can rely.

Make a good discovery with the BEBEDC method.

Please note: once the relationship of trust is established, your job does not end there. You have to keep your promise. Develop an efficient after-sales service, a follow-up that allows you to retain your customer. Give him important assistant he needs to use your solution and succeed in achieving his goal.

For example, prepare tutorials or help sections for your technical solutions. Send order picking and shipping tracking emails / SMS for your products. Make reminders of your interventions in physics, of your installations—progress points in the deployment of your solution, visits to check that everything is working, etc.

By keeping a regular link with your customers, you will more easily discuss business topics and more easily understand any future signals.

1. Analyze your actions

Measure everything you do! This is the shortest way to identify dysfunctions and remedy them, especially when you are just starting out. We are lucky to have some business. A number of calls, number of site visits, customer conversion rate, progress year by year...

Remember the purpose you set at the starting of this article. Now, compare your current performance with them. Ask yourself a question:

- Will, I hit my numbers at this pace?
- Do my negotiation techniques allow me to transform my prospects into clients?

If not, the best moment to revisit your sales methods and identify the source of the loophole.

Above all, don't wait until it's too late to hit your numbers. It is a mistake that I have made for a long time. "I am going to get over it, I give it a boost, and it will pass." Sometimes it's hard to question yourself and face the truth: what I'm doing isn't working ...

All great athletes go through this. They analyze each of their performance from all angles. They spare themselves nothing. If you measure everything you do, you will be able to identify obstacles and resolve issues as they arise. Correct things on time, experiment with new sales methods to understand what works and what to stop doing.

For example, if you see that you are missing information (price, deadlines, etc.) at the end of an appointment, it is because your discovery questions must be found. With the QCP method, you will no longer be able to miss it.

Don't hesitate to ask your managers or the salespeople around you for help. Feedback from the field is always the best. But do it before it's too late.

2. **Sell to the right targets**

How many of us are exhausted trying to convince customers who will never be? Haven't you persevered in a sale with a prospect who you knew deep down had no potential?
Early in my professional life, I invested a lot of time contacting and prospecting people who didn't want to talk to me. But over the past five years, I've spent more time meeting people who want to hear what I have to say. I just learned to target my audience.

Buyer persona creation template

Who are the typical customers of my business? Those who sign up most often for my products? Function, sector, decision-making power ... By building what we call your buyers personas, that is to say, the description of your ideal client, you will better target your actions and know in advance who is more likely to sign.

Encourage information sharing

When you are new to selling, you want to be successful in your industry. Many salespeople think the fastest way to do this is to eliminate the "competition" (that is, the rest of their team).
They have it all wrong. This method can even be detrimental.

This approach is insulating, and you will lose a lot. Regardless of your level of experience, the lone wolf is out of place in the current sales cycle. Customers need collective intelligence to find a viable solution. Salespeople can no longer work alone, and the new generation does not want it. She seeks collaboration, a team spirit, benevolent competition. Cohesion is a strength in a sales team.
For example, if you are trying unsuccessfully to reach the CEO of a large corporation, ask around if someone doesn't have him in their network or know of a middleman.

In my sales force, we have been operating like this for a few years. It took a long time - a lot of time even - so that everyone no longer looks at their own backyard but thinks collectively and feels that a helping hand will inevitably be given later. We more often share on the fly our difficulties during negotiations, complicated prospecting calls. Everyone gives their opinion to help the other to progress and feels comfortable doing so.

When you're a salesperson, you think you have to solve everything on your own that we are the only ones who can find the ideal solution to everything, use your team's expertise more often to close your offers! Along the way, you'll learn valuable skills and soon realize that every salesperson has the knowledge to share.

A word of advice => Take the time, every week, or every month, to listen to how your teammates lead successful sales calls. Whether you are listening live or listening to recordings, you can come up with key phrases/words, techniques for building a customer relationship, and closing strategies ... which you can use and personalize during your next calls.

Learn from calls from other salespeople

Your manager has most likely trained you on how to pitch over the phone and surely gives you booster shots from time to time. But is it enough? Are you really comfortable on the phone?
Yet, it is the beginning of everything. If you are not impactful on the phone, it will be difficult for us to make appointments and then get your client to sign.

Identify the qualities of the salespeople around you (the one who excels in going through a roadblock, the one who knows how to deal with all objections, the one for whom customer follow-up has no secrets, etc.).

Do you appreciate a salesperson with excellent negotiation skills? Ask him to review your recent negotiations. Amplify different aspects of calls and meetings and perform precise analysis to improve each part. Identify what you can improve and do better. All you have to do is apply.

The very precious advice I can give you is to learn from your colleagues today, tomorrow, and today, ten years later. Continuous learning will make you an excellent salesperson. This is what makes the sales business flourish.

Chapter # 6

The First 90 Days

My first 90 days salesman by experience

I will share my work experience as a new salesman, my first 90 -day experience. I fell in love with the work I did, and I was very good at it. But I am not good at the beginning. I was not good at sales, 9 to 5 work schedules, a fixed salary, a desk, a dress code, or any other conditions that come with a traditional full-time work structure. I always wanted to be my boss since when I was born, and when I was in my late teens, I got my first sales job. And I wanted to succeed in it. Not only that, but I wanted to thrive in it. After three months, and a lot of research, I completed my goal by following some great rules, which I will tell you in this book.

I didn't know what I was doing, and I didn't save money -all I know is that I want to achieve this goal of becoming a good salesperson.

Because if I do not want to make a robust and risky decision that would change my career path, who will? When am I? I was 19 years old and have no wife, children, or mortgage. If there is time to take a risk, it is now.

The following three months were full of ups and downs, as I was a new salesman and didn't know much about this job, but I have been listening, learning, participating, and practicing. I am not confident, but with "fake goods until the success of "old thinking, I've been with the potential customer to keep in touch with their families and signed. Even if I don't think I" deserve "it, I have been raising interest rates. Even when I week people around to tell me I'm crazy, I move on.

I recall push income salesman, and within three months, I realized income had increased two-fold.
My income ratio is more boss-time jobs, and I know most of the Fresh Salesman is true.
I have been following their terms and their own time to complete all the work. That's great.
Something actual proof, I am not the only one trapped in a full-time job, the limitations, frustrated and bored people. Therefore, I will teach you the benefits I gained in three months and the measures to achieve my goals. Here are some secrets that I want to tell you about my first 90 days of experience.

1. Change your mindset and confidence level

The majority of Fresh salesman, tend to push and due to inexperience, fail. I have been guided by the idea that this was their own business, but this was the first big mistake I made because it's not. I mean, partially. Let me explain:
For my boss, on his point of view, I mean two things:

First, his goal was to not forget to take into consideration the company's point of view, rather than making decisions from the perspective of individual operators. For example, employees are accustomed to other people making decisions for them and following specific directions. On the other hand, entrepreneurs and business owners must be proactive, constantly aware of their next move, and be ready to jump into the new situation at any time. If you continue to treat yourself and your company as employees, all your work will plummet.

Also, attention is needed to the terminology you use, such as saying "my vacation" or "waiting for a reply," the kind of thing rooted in negative emotions. You are no longer a passive employee but a business owner.

Also, when someone starts their own business when the industry, it will ask you to remain switched on and always own the next step. However, if you change your mindset unconsciously, it will not happen.

Second, you will have to re-establish confidence. As for the Fresh Salesman, I have used others before actually verifying our actions and beliefs. We need the consent of others to make the right decision. Wrong.

As a self-starter, we do not have the time, patience, or interest in the ideas of others. No matter how people say, you have to be 100 % believe in yourself and in the next step to take action in the effort. Execution is the key, not perfection.

Before conducting business, you must make sure you have the right attitude; otherwise, it is tough to develop and grow.

2. Identify your most profitable Products

Once you get rid of the shackles of stereotypes, it's time to start researching your business. The 1st step in doing this is to look at aspects of your innate good - anything else in waves fee for your time.

Most new fresh salesman brainwashed that you will eventually do better in this regard if you continue to do something. Guys, but guess if this is true? Instead, focus on what the talent is and what is inherently better than others. No, not your continuous efforts or willingness to do or hope for the better future of things - it looks like you better at other people's things, and people respond to you. These are things you should fully invest in, nothing more.

And even if you are not good at all the other things that must occur long? (For example, taxation .) Outsource it.

A small but essential tip: When you view your strengths, do not ask yourself: "My excellence of what is that? "

Why? Because you can't find anything. It isn't easy to find a personal quality worthy of an American president or celebrity status. This is why most of us are not American presidents or celebrities, but it does not mean that we cannot get high salaries for our excellent work. Instead, focus on what you are better at than others. That's it.

To figure this out, ask yourself some questions, such as:

People who will praise me what?
"Wow, your apartment decorated so well - how do you know how to do that? "

People have asked me what?
"Hey, I work in mathematics encountered trouble in the industry; I know you're good at math - can you help me complete this operation? "

What is my valuable experience with others?
"Wait, you little time to live in Mexico, speaks fluent Spanish? Can you teach me ?!"
This is a compelling and straightforward way to identify your product and see what others have said about you. Never pursue a business idea that you are inherently incapable of because it will fail. Pursue only what you are good at and discard everything else. If you do, you will be unstoppable.

3. To find the intersection between the product, interest, and demand points
Just kidding ... You can not just pursue your good at something long. Because what if you hate it?

For example, I'm good at long sales, because I am a person, but I wouldn't like deals. Maybe someone else can be a mathematician, but they will not enjoy the coaching business if they despise math.

Therefore, the project objective is to find something you like and your point of intersection between the skilled product of things. That is a good place for you.

4. Make sure your goal mark by the public

Of course, when selling products or services, you cannot target *everyone*.

If you try to sell products to everyone, you will not sell off-key to make the target audience as specific as possible and dialogue with their roles.

For example, if I want to sell skin care products, I can't target every woman who gets facial care.

Conversely, many of those people I would go for the treatment of acne: 13 to 20 - year-old woman, suffering from cystic / steroid-induced acne sore, tired of trying to one million kinds of ineffective products.

5. Pass through your brand content share price value

No one will see the first time you post or hear the advertisement about you and will not immediately buy the product you are selling (unless this is a cure for cancer or another way that can completely change your life, and is The only way).

With social media, smartphones, and millions of other dry interference factors, you have to find a way to attract their attention and build trust with them before buying goods.

6. The establishment of a superclass organized schedule so that you will stick with

Okay, take a deep breath. This time, your position correct, your business idea is ready, the site has been established, it is time to open the store. However, if you and several passengers contracted households, and you suddenly into a Salesman in confusion, then the navigation will be complicated. Therefore, it is better to be organized initially, not to be collected at the beginning.

The salesman who fails is the one who wakes up every morning and has no plan for the day. Your entire week - everyone Shi - should be planned before the start of Sunday. It does not have to contain all the details, but it should include a consistent period so that you can focus on your tasks every day.

How to stay organized is up to you, but if you plan carefully, you may become the boss, doing a lot of work frantically every day. It all depends on you.

7. Continually master your craft

Just because you are a certain kind of consultant, coach, or service provider now does not make you the king of the world. You don't know anything.

Check yourself constantly and determine how you can develop and improve your market segment. Maybe you can set aside time every morning to read industry-related publications and blogs, make connections and learn from others in your field, or practice your work (if you are a writing coach, it's best to keep your Writing habits to maintain one's level). For example, your mind is sharp).

There will always be more things to learn, and the more knowledge and experience you have, the more you can charge customers. Therefore, please set aside time every day, week, or month to study your field of expertise in more depth and track your progress.

I guarantee a card, which will be rewarded.

8. Join the conversation

Well, it's time to start sharing your information with the world. Depending on who your target audience is, it may be best to focus more on specific social media platforms.

But not on where they live; they are beginning to join related online groups, forums, and dialogues involving the target audience. For example, perhaps the Facebook group set, Reddit population group, or Twitter thread.

However, off-key not immediately start promoting your product. You will be blocked almost immediately.

Instead, start a conversation. Respond to people's comments, ask questions and provide feedback.

Accurate, relevant and build relationships. Then, after a few days, you should talk about your products. But only after establishing a connection.

9. Create a lead capture automation system

As is an entrepreneur, you have only one person a day, only 24- Xiao Shi. This means that you cannot work with everyone at once (if you are a good salesman, many people will try).

However, things get tricky: you may meet many people in your freelance career who might want to work with you in the future. But until then, you didn't want to ignore them. What if they forget you? Or hire someone else? What if you forget them? To keep them in touch and do business with your salesperson, please start emailing them.

Chapter # 7

Pitfalls and How to Avoid Them

To be distracted

By giving the prospect your full attention, you will, in turn, gain the prospect's full attention.

Recently a young salesperson came to my office by appointment. He gave a rather long speech on his product; I am sitting in silence. He got to a point where he had been instructed to ask his prospect a few questions. He asked them conscientiously but with a specific stiffness as if reciting a speech. Time and time again, as I started to answer him, I noticed the salesperson staring into space, paying no attention to what I was saying. He might as well have taken a coffee break. Maybe he wanted to.

Many salespeople are so busy writing their to-do checklist that they forget they're dealing with another human being and start focusing on things that have nothing to do with selling.

Part of the reason for this has to do with the stress associated with selling for a living. Often, when faced with a stressful situation, we lock ourselves into a small, comfortable world of our own - a world that we can usually control but carries the genuine risk of missing something important.

It is estimated that the average salesperson sells less than five and a half hours a week. In other meanings, if you're like most salespeople, you aren't selling every hour of every day. You do something else: prepare to see prospects, place your prospecting calls, write proposals, attend meetings, fill out documents, etc. That's why it's so vital to make sure that every minute you spend with a prospect count. As a result, you need to focus on what is being said; don't dream, and don't get distracted.

When you get distracted on a sales call, you distract your prospect. You start to get restless; you wonder what there is for lunch; you think about the movie you are going to tonight; you let your mind wander when it shouldn't be wandering. It ruins the whole meeting because your prospect will sense what's going on and wonder what's wrong. The atmosphere of trust will not materialize - and that's terrible news. It would help if you had that confidence.

If you need an incentive, remember that, directly or indirectly, the prospect tells you the most important thing you'll hear all day: whether or not they'll buy your product and why.

Take notes to help you focus; make sure your briefcase is well organized, with everything you need close at hand. The tools you bring with you to the meeting should help, not hinder you. If you spend five minutes fishing a brochure out of your suitcase, something is wrong.

The same idea applies to the common problem of attaching too much importance to a confusing or negative remark from the prospect. If the candidate tells you that the left is the right and the right is the left, don't be confused, don't ask for an explanation, and by all means, challenge the person. What will you gain? Politely ask for clarification if any of them seem in order, then sit back and pick up where you left off.

Try to get a pearl on the interests and personality of the prospect. Ask your basic questions. Then repeat the prospect's ideas. ("So, what I hear is that your main concerns are ...")
If so, let the prospect take the lead and pay attention to what happens next. By isolating the factors unique to that particular perspective, you will remind yourself that you are dealing with another person - someone important enough to pay close attention to.

Don't take notes

As I briefly mentioned earlier, taking proper notes will help you keep the prospect's needs in mind and improve your presentation.

All sales can be broken down into four stages: prospecting, interviewing, presenting, and closing. Perhaps the most crucial step in selling is the second: the interview. This is where you learn what precisely the prospect's needs and wants are and whether or not your product or service can help solve a pressing problem. Note-taking is an essential part of this process, and it's a lingering mystery why so many people fail to use this important sales tool.

Suppose I have already taken the prospecting step by contacting you by cold call. Let's say I come to your office now for a sales appointment. You and I meet. We shake hands. You tell me to sit down. I do. You're looking at me; I'm looking at you. We exchange a little conversation, learn a little about each other, and establish common points. As the meeting progresses in this manner, there will come a time when you will look at me and say, in one form or another, those words that so many salespeople have come to dread.

"Well - what can I do for you?"

This is where the real work begins. How can I handle this first transition can create or split my sales call? Luckily, I have a notepad and a pen. These tools will help me build a solid and professional relationship with you.

In response, I say to you, "Well, Mrs. Jones, I work for ABC Widgets. We're the largest widget maker on the East Coast, and we've worked with about 15 companies in your industry. And the cause I wanted to talk to you today was to find out if there was anything we could do to work together to increase your production. I had a few questions for you on this subject. Is everything alright? "

And I take out my notepad and my pen. Automatically, I made a statement. Just by doing so much, I have shown you that I am a professional; I am organized; I control; and, most importantly, I am concerned about your interests (increasing production).

You say, "Of course; go ahead."

And I keep asking you questions about the past, present, and future when it comes to your use of widgets.

Note that I'm not responding to your "what can I do for you" line when talking about the beauty of my Model X widget. I can't do that yet. I don't know enough about you. I am still at the interview stage. So, I have to find out more about what you need - and you get to talk about yourself and your business - by asking questions and taking notes.

Now here is the exciting part. Anyone who uses this technique for a while will find that prospects speak more when you have a pen and a notepad than they will if you ask them to point-blank and ignore taking notes. Your book-taking reinforces the prospect's desire to talk, and that, of course, gives you more to write about. It is a self-sustaining cycle.

Give it a try. You will find that it works like nothing else on earth. Why? The fact that I take notes dramatizes my role as a collector of information. This makes my job very clear to you, the prospect: I am here to know your needs.

It's a bit flattering, isn't it? It shows that I care what you say and how you look at things. And as long as I'm taking the trouble to write it all down, you'll want to make sure I have the correct information about your business and its issues with widgets, right?

Because I consider the issue to be a significant issue, you will agree that it is essential for me to know your widget needs. And you know what? You will be correct. It is important. Getting this information is the only way I can help you solve your problem.

Involve the prospect; to take notes. Use the right tools: A hard-backed legal pad and a sleek gold ballpoint pen can make a big impression. (Fountain pens, while dramatic, can leak and stain your writing.) Stay away from the envelopes or bulky pad/wallet sets; it will harm the professional image you are trying to present.

Make your prospective clients feel as important as a political candidate for an interview with a movie star or a press conference. Then, in the subsequent stages of your sales, use the collected information to determine your approach.

Do not keep in touch with former clients

This fits perfectly with Mistake, of course, where we talked about staying in touch with prospects and current customers. The basic idea here is that someone who decides to use your product or service and then falls out of your existing customer base is probably still a highly qualified prospect.

Help customers keep you in mind. Importantly, if a significant amount of time has passed (and it can range from a few months to several years), old customers will often come to a point where they will need your product or service again but will not remember how to get back. In touch with you!

When a salesperson first calls you and gives you their contact information, do you instantly enter that information into your address book? Probably not. It's usually salespeople's job to remind potential customers - tactfully and professionally - that the salesperson's business is still out there and producing great results. Don't harass people to death but give old clients all the information they need to work with you again.

It is estimated that you have a one in two chance of doing business from an existing account and a one in four cases of doing business from an old version. When looking for new customers, the odds drop to one in twenty. Without diminishing by a minute the importance of attracting new customers, you can see that staying in touch with your old customers is a high income for you. Keep an organized file of inactive accounts; regularly call or write to key people in these companies. Don't do this in an intrusive or unprofessional way - just keep in touch, professional to professional.

This approach doesn't have to be an intrusive "hard sell," nor does it have to be the rapid pace that many salespeople bring to their prospecting work. After all, you already have a co-operation with the person. Keep Calm, Stay Friendly, and Be Professional. Don't rush things. If the person is not able to buy now, come back in a month or two.

You might want to set up a simple database system to keep track of your contacts. (By the way, that last sentence originally started, "If you have access to a personal computer and are proficient at a computer ..." I might need to update these books more often.) Just make sure that you don't get carried away with the process - when you spend more time in front of a computer screen than in front of your prospects, something is wrong. Start small and work your way up.

Don't fall in love with a computer or BlackBerry just because it's a computer or BlackBerry. Make it work for you. Remember, high tech that doesn't urgently help you achieve your goals isn't high tech at all - it's probably bad tech.

We are not planning the day effectively

Think for a moment about Mistake # 1; it's relevant here. You have to be determined to get the most out of your day, and daily planning is one of them. Let's face it. Committing to a daily schedule is paramount; your success or failure in this area will significantly impact your overall performance as a salesperson.

Now there are many books on time management. Unfortunately, most of them are so complicated and take so long to read (not to mention implementation) that they are virtually worthless to most sellers today. In this section, we'll take a look at some brief ideas that you can instantly incorporate into your daily routine - so you can start seeing results early in business tomorrow.

Don't waste hours; you might be talking to clients. Plan your day the day before.

Prioritize your goals. Don't just start filling a schedule willy-nilly one night; Make a list of all the things you want to accomplish, then rank them in order of importance before including them in your plan.

Allow time for crises. Planning to the brim every day will get you off your plan. We all know that weird and unpredictable problems can crop up from time to time. Leave an hour or two open at the end of the day to deal with sudden difficulties. If no crisis arises, you can always move on to your next priority item.

Get up fifteen minutes earlier than now - and give yourself a positive energy charge during the extra time. Starting the day in a rush hurts things off to a bad start. Start the day with a positive affirmation: "It's going to be a great day." Eat a good breakfast. Listen to pleasant music. Avoid reading or listening to the news in the morning; It's too depressing. Be kind to yourself. (Don't worry, it won't last long.)

Buy and use the doctor's appointment book - the kind of whole day marked in fifteen-minute increments. Next, keep a close eye on how much time you spend on any given item. This research will help you avoid the temptation to allocate significant portions of your day to loosely defined goals when putting together your to-do list.

Also, buy a second, smaller book, which can fit in your pocket or purse. Here you will be recording what you are doing during the day. Nothing extravagant; just a quick note of the time for each project you take on as you work all day. The beauty of this is that you end up with a written record of events, not just your plans, and you can compare the two at the end of the day. If there's a massive gap between what you plan for 6 p.m. Tuesday and what you did on Wednesday at 6 p.m., you'll know it and can work on it. If you are like most salespeople, you will probably realize how much time you spend on the road. Chances are, you'll acquire a new enthusiasm for quality date scheduling. You'll also have hard evidence of your habits - having lunch at a particular time, so many calls in the morning, so much downtime between meetings, etc. By knowing this "data," your daily planning will become much more efficient.

On Friday evening, prepare not only your Monday morning schedule but also your small sketch for the week ahead. Most likely, this will take the form of meetings and other engagements; don't feel like you have to account for every minute of each of the next five days. Simply block your scheduled appointments and meetings to get a good overview of what's on the horizon. If necessary, leave - you "in Labrador OUT- of "time. After all, you know that you won't just materialize from scratch at your three-hour rendezvous across town, but you'll need to get there by car, leaving early enough to ensure the arrival of around ten minutes, before three o'clock.

By conscientiously dealing with daily planning issues and comparing your actual results with your plan, you will increase your time efficiency and lay a solid foundation for your business success.

Don't organize sales tools.

Your professional image, as we have seen, depends to a large extent on your appearance. However, you should also keep in mind that it also depends on your tools.
What do you think of a prospect who, after meeting a salesperson, sees all kinds of objects randomly fall out of their open briefcase?

Your briefcase should give an impression of order and precision when opened. It shouldn't be overflowing with laundry lists, last week's newspapers, dirty ties, bills, or food.

It should contain your legal notepad, your business cards; your thinking; appropriate product materials and samples; a portable calculator, and maybe your pocket planner. That's it.
Often, salespeople bring too much to date. You don't need everything in the building to speak to a single prospect, and while carrying reams of samples and brochures may make you feel more secure on the way to the appointment, you will probably look confused and puzzled. Paw through it all, trying to find the material you want.

If your type of sale requires the display of a tangible product, you will need to incorporate that element, perhaps with a brilliant case example. But stay away from fancy flip charts, presentation boxes, and framed testimonials. They almost always pose more problems than they are worth. Usually, the only thing you can count on from all this foreign material is a less confident and balanced presentation.

If you find that you go to your appointments so loaded with samples and showcase that you are exhausted the minute you walk in the door, you may have to make a change somewhere. If it is agony for you to carry all of this, it will be agony for the prospect of looking at you. Try to identify areas of the prospect's concern; you can always bring the material requested on your second visit.

As we will learn later in this book, a business can be compared, in many ways, to war. Both require strategy, planning, competition, intelligence, etc. If you think of your sales job in this way, you will find that your sales tools are genuinely part of your ammunition. As such, they should be maintained with care and respect.

Don't be proud of your work.

A few years ago, I went to do a program at a large consumer products company. During a question-and-answer period, I asked participants to indicate the reasons why their company should be considered number one in its field.

I was standing there in front of the flip chart, marker in hand, waiting. No answer. After a while, a hand rose. "And it's?" AI, I asked. "You know, Steve," the man says (and I'm paraphrasing him here), "we might be number one on taxi-late widgets, but when it comes to looking at the global production of midsize devices, I think we get around number four."

"No," a woman shouted from the back of the room. "No, six. Mid-sized widgets, we just got the new ranking; we're sixth."

"Sixth," the man said.

Another break.

"Okay, that's interesting to know," I said. "Nothing else? What makes this company great? Nobody?"

A man in the front row cleared his throat.

"And it's?"

"The new cafeteria," he said slowly, "is undoubtedly lovely.

Just then, a young man asked to be recognized.

"And that is? What is it that motivates you about this business?"

I looked surprised. "What?" I asked. "Oh no, I just wanted to say something. Mort mentioned the cafeteria. They had some plumbing issues; I just thought I would let everyone know it was out of service this week.

"So, I will resume," said Mort, "what I said about the cafeteria.

"You know what bothers me," said a young woman to my right, "it's the way they've changed the pay schedules. We used to get reviews every year on January 1st. They do this before your anniversary date with the company, which means I'll have a raise six weeks later this year. "

You see my point. The group I was speaking to had not seen it as an article of faith to be proud of in their organization. Instead, when asked to list the positive aspects of their work environment, they either made minor complaints or said nothing at all.

This is not the way to make your business number one, nor is it the way to become number one.

If you can't support what you're doing and where you're doing it with every fiber of your being, why bother? Why punches a clock? Why show up in the morning? Why does something that you don't like to do? Why ask people to buy your product or service if you don't believe it?

If you are not proud of your product or service and the organization that supports it, you will not be successful. If you just focus on the negatives, the obstacles, the reasons why you can't sell the way you should - guess what? You will not sell as you should.

Identify the factors that set you apart from your competition. Be comfortable optimistically discussing these factors. In short, talk about your organization. Don't just do this at work, although it's undoubtedly essential there, but mention where you work and why it's great at parties, social gatherings, conventions - everywhere. (By the way, this will not only boost your optimism about the business but also expose you to a whole new world of potential customers.)

Now. Suppose you have a real problem with your business. Suppose the reason you don't feel good about your work goes beyond regular sales cycles or standard management headaches and instead is rooted in a legitimate, profound objection. As if you have a moral problem selling what you are selling. Or a supervisor engages in persistent, subtle (or maybe not so subtle) sexual harassment. Or the quotas you have to meet are so high that all staff regularly run out and the turnover rate is always high.

Does that mean you shouldn't be excited about where you work?

No. This means that you should be excited about where you work, but you should be working elsewhere.

If you can't support the program 100%, find a place where you can - then give it all you have. Be proud of where you work and what you do for a living. You will see that the results will follow soon.

I was trying to convince rather than transmitting.
When you want to make a sale - I mean, desperately want to make a sale - it's easy to go into a "convincing" mode. You corner the prospect, you will examine why your product or service is excellent, you will overcome any annoying objections, and finally, the candidate will emerge and buy from you.

The only problem is, it's the exact opposite of what you need to do. You need to be committed to understanding the prospect's issues and concerns, not controlling them. And you have to work from there to show - to convincingly demonstrate - how your product or service can address relevant problems.

In short, you need to convey value and benefit rather than convincing the prospect that their concerns are unfounded. Remember: it's always better to let the candidate speak and act on the voicing circumstances than to do all the talking yourself and wait for a positive response.

I know it is essential for you to make sales. That's the whole idea behind the work I do and behind every word in this book. But most successful salespeople find that being anxious to close a sale and working like crazy to get the prospect to see your point of view will only decrease your chances of closing.

Sales are not about getting other people to see your point of view. It's about making you see things from other people's perspectives. If you're committed to helping your prospect solve a problem, "convincing" doesn't matter.

The problem isn't changing someone's mind but explaining why and how you can help solve an urgent situation. And you have to see and understand this problem before you can hope to fix it.
That's not to say that high-pressure manipulative selling doesn't exist. It does. But think about how you felt the last time you had something "thrown in your throat" by a high-pressure salesperson. Did it make you feel better about the company the salesperson was working for? Did it

make you want to go back for another purchase? Did it make you want to recommend the company to others?

The critical question you need to ask yourself is: are you interested in developing a career in sales, or are you interested in creating a deal?

When people have been overwhelmed by a salesperson, when they have doubts about the wisdom of a buying decision, when they fear they've been cheated, they say, "A salesperson sold me this. "When people feel excellent about a product, they say, "I bought this." It's the difference between a one-time sale and a good, solid customer. Which would you prefer to have?

Build trust. Highlight past successes. Highlight solutions to problems. By doing this, you will convey the points necessary to get the prospect to make the right decisions.

They are not keeping up to date

Knowledge is power.

Suppose you walked in to see a current client for a meeting, and your contact has lost an arm since you last saw them. Would you notice it?

Indeed, something so obvious probably wouldn't escape you. However, from a prospect's business perspective, some hints and tips are just as straightforward - directions visible when you walk in the door, but many salespeople miss them.

What is happening in your clients' businesses? Do you know? If there was a significant layoff insight, would you hear about it? Is the company doing well? Is a merger in progress? Are vital people happy with your product or service, or is it something a budget shredder might consider consumable?

Too many salespeople tend to think of "closed sales" as static, and very few in business are. The sad truth is that no company exists for the sole purpose of buying your product or service. If your clients are doing well, you will be doing well - and, conversely, if they are doing poorly, you will be doing poorly. In any case, it is to your advantage to have precise information in advance.

Observing the prospect closely, making an effort to understand precisely what is going on in their business (and why) will help you gain a broader view of the entire environment in which your business operates.

Of course, observing your prospects first-hand isn't the only weapon at your disposal. There are countless reports, reviews, and newsletters available to you - and if you have a lot of clients in a given industry, it's a good idea to keep up with business news from that industry.

A salesperson I know named Marcia had tried to get in touch with someone at a large company about their company's courier service. She was not going anywhere, and when her contact asked her to "send information," she was convinced she was at a dead end. Yet she dutifully sent the information, but nothing happened for weeks. She wrote off the account.

Six months later, she received a call from her contact at the firm. Could she come for a date right away? She could and did and made a big sale. Curios- it has got the better of her, however, and at the end of the meeting, she came to the right and wondered why they had waited so long to respond? The answer: The company's main competitor launched a new program earlier that year that required courier service. They were getting down to it now and wished they knew what their rivals were doing earlier.

The moral, of course, is that if Marcia had been able to keep up with industry posts and gossip, she might well have told her contact how a courier worked for others in the industry. - and closed the account. Months earlier.

Who is your prospect selling to? Who are your prospect's competitors? How do these competitors sell? What are the main differences between the products and prices of your prospect's business and its competitors? What is the prospect's market share? What is the prospect's perceived market share? How does your prospect plan to deal with the new obstacles? New opportunities? Are there new technological breakthroughs on the horizon? How do all of these factors affect decisions about whether or not to buy from you?

Avoid unnecessarily complex and tedious research, but keep your eyes and ears open and read essential publications. The more you know, the better off you will be.

Rushing to sell

I mentioned earlier that there are four stages to every sale. We'll take a closer look at these four steps here. No matter what you are selling or where you are selling it, your deal can usually be broken down into the following stages: qualification, interview, presentation, and close. Let's have a look at each step one by one.

Qualification. Also called prospecting or cold calling, this is where you contact someone you have never spoken to before (often by calling them on the phone) and determine that there is a possible use for your product. or service. You can schedule an appointment or a date for the next call at this point.

To interview. You learn about the past, present, and future related to the prospect's use of your product or service. You find out what particular problems have arisen recently. You learn other relevant facts about the opportunity.

Presentation. You show exactly how your product or service can help solve the problems identified during the maintenance phase. You appeal to past successes with other clients.

Closing. You ask for the sale.

You may be able to go through all four steps in one phone call. It's also possible that it may take you months, or even years, of appointments and follow-up appointments to go from cold calling to the endgame. It all matters on the product or service you offer, your industry, customers, the prevailing economic conditions - several different factors.

At some point in the cycle, your goal is to move from where you are to the next step. In other words, if you qualify, your goal is to go for the interview; if you are interviewing, you want to get to a point where the prospect is comfortable with a presentation, and so on. However, there is one rule that you should keep in mind when considering the cycles I described above. The rule is simple: the easiest and most reliable way to lose a sale is to jump through the stages before the prospect is ready to do so.

Many salespeople see their work as a gigantic closing stage. By not understanding the cyclical nature of their work with a prospect, they rush things and, as a result, lose sales.

Let's say you have a garden. One morning you go out to your garden and sow seeds for a tomato plant. If you are an intelligent gardener, you will find that it will take most of the summer for the tomato to move from the seed stage to your salad bowl. If you wait a few weeks, see something that vaguely resembles a tomato emerge from the ground, tear it up, and smother it with dressing, it won't make a delicious (even edible) salad.

However, if you give it time and let it ripen, it will blossom into a juicy, ripe tomato. Then you can brag about it. But if you rush the process, you won't get anything for your efforts.

Selling is the same. You have to wait; otherwise, you are not in the business; you are in the rejection realm. You are a professional collector of rejections.

You don't have to try to walk into an office for the first time, shake a prospect's hand, and ask when the operations department wants to receive the first order. In this case, you are trying to move quickly from the maintenance phase to the final step, and your results will be disastrous. Most of the precipitation issues, however, are not so obvious. Maybe you've talked a little bit about yourself, mentioned your product, taken in the view, had a bit of a story, and been assured that what you're talking about "looks interesting."

Are you ready to move on to the presentation stage? Maybe - and maybe not. The best option is usually to ask the prospect directly, "Is there anything else you think I should know about your business, Mr. Smith?" Based on the response you get; you'll be able to gauge the prospect's enthusiasm for taking the next step. When in doubt, be patient. It is no crime to say, "Well, I learned a lot about your business today; what I would like to do now is set an appointment for next week so that I can go over a full proposal with you. "

Do not use proof of people.

What is proof of persons?

"Mr. Jones, I know this program will work for you, and I'll tell you why. We had a company in your industry, ABC Tires, that was very skeptical of what we said we could do for them. But they tried the program, and we delivered the results. And I know the same can happen here with your business."

It's people-proof, and it's one of the most potent ammunition available to you. People proof reinforces positive inclinations towards your business and gives people a logical reason to uphold the emotional decision to do business. If you can name another company (or better yet, another company in the same industry) that has had success with the product or service you are now offering, you are well on your way to building the confidence to close the deal. Comes out.

Many salespeople react badly when I make this suggestion. They say, "Steve, this won't work for me; I work in an industry where confidentiality is essential."

I have news for you. Everyone works in an industry where confidentiality is essential.

This is a simple enough question to erase such informal use of client names in advance. After all, you are not divulging company secrets but simply revealing that you worked for a particular company. You do the same thing when you type in a customer list.

Just tell your contact at ABC Tires that you would like to be able to include their company (and maybe even their name, please) in your literature and personal presentations. Keep the atmosphere relaxed and friendly; don't give the impression that your client is making any commitment to you. You might be surprised by the results. The client's typical reaction is to be flattered, not paranoid.

People's evidence works wonders. That makes you less of an untested amount and more of a proven problem solver.

It builds legitimacy in the prospect's eyes and helps you focus on the critical task of solving problems with your product or service.

Humiliate oneself

Are you a professional? There is no need for you to demean yourself or misunderstand a prospect rather than working with the person to solve a problem. This usually has a negative effect - rather than a positive one - on your sales efforts.

During a program I was running some time ago, I recommended a saleswoman named Myra to meet her contact at a particular company and arrange a meeting with the manager. The company. She was shocked at this suggestion.

"Oh, Steve," she said. "I can't do this."
"Why not?" Ai, I asked.

"Well," she explained, "if I ask my interviewer to put me in touch with the president, the answer might be no. So, where would I be with my contact? "

There's a new idea, don't you think? A salesperson faced with the word "no" - indeed a once-in-a-lifetime event in a salesperson's life, and certainly a great reason not to try something in the first place.

Myra, I learned, was not in the business three months later. Why not? Well, think about it. In this exchange, she and I had talked a lot about how she viewed her contact - and selling as a profession. She was petrified at the thought of offending her touch, and I guess it was because she believed, deep down, that the communication was doing her a favour by giving her stuff.

In short, she gave up control of her sales environment and humbled herself towards contacts. His thought was probably turning to something like this: if I'm nice enough to Mrs. Jones if I take her out to lunch every week if I remember the names and dates of her children's births if I never give her one. Reason to have a free meal, open, trade with me - if I can do all of that, maybe, just maybe, I'll be on her side enough for her to buy me a widget.

Something is missing there, don't you think?
Where did Ms. Jones' company need widgets come from? And where does Myra's role as an intermediary and facilitator come in?

I guess Myra cannot see itself as a professional-as partner. On the contrary, Myra of this world tends to see himself as a supplicant.

Are you a professional? Or are you still trying to win the respect of professionals from potential customers? Paradoxically, simply striving for this kind of respect can distract people from what you are saying.

Of course, the way you look at yourself has a lot to do with the way other people look at you. This is why a commitment to continuous motivational work is so important.

No one says sales are straightforward. No one is saying that you will never be rejected. And no one is saying that there won't be days when you feel like you haven't achieved anything no matter how hard you try.

Still, you need to find an internal reservoir of strength, confidence, and security in your professional identity. You need to convey all of this to your prospect - as an equal. Because that's what you are.
You have to assume that you bring to the table a specific set of skills and a level of product knowledge that the other person can benefit from. If you go on the opposite assumption, that the person in front of you has a prize that you can win if only you can prove that you are worthy of him or her, you are in trouble. The only people you're going to win (if you're lucky) are extremely insecure prospects - and these aren't the people who tend to achieve the highest levels of business success.

When you stop to think about it, I'll bet you'll find that the people you'll most want to work with (and emulate) have a strong sense of self, confidence, and professionalism - and have all the expectations of—the same of you.

Don't let them down.

Take rejection personally
After discussing, in the previous chapter, how you make money when someone says 'no,' we're in an excellent position to take a closer look at the whole issue of rejection and how salespeople respond to it.

For a salesperson, as we have seen, rejection is not a personal affront but rather part of the overall cycle inherent in any working day.

Salespeople just have to learn to look at the problem this way. After all, there's only one surefire way to avoid rejection - even if it works like a charm. This way, you should never ask for anything. Don't ask for an appointment; do not ask for the sale; don't try to show your prospect how you can help solve problems. You will never be rejected. Unfortunately, you will never make any money either.

A man I worked with recently, Frank, was trying to make the transition from being an administrator to being a field sales representative. He entered the new post with high hopes. After all, he was a human person. He loved to talk about his product. And he knew it inside and out.

However, he was not prepared for the work he had to do to make his efforts worthwhile. He quickly learned to arrive at a realistic number of "yes" answers, and he had to be prepared to listen to many "no" solutions. And it was hard for him.

Frank had worked for fifteen years in a different environment. He had gotten used to working for weeks on a proposal, pushing that proposal through and coming back to him with suggestions, then preparing another project - a project everyone believed in.

Now he was wondering how to move from that slow, consensus-driven work to a fast-firing, binary, on-or-off world that deeply troubled him.

He said to me, "Steve, it's not about not knowing that rejection is part of the cycle. I know how many people I have to see to make money; that's the number of people I see. And I'm fine. But I am completely stressed out. I guess it's more of a problem for me to believe that they refuse me when people refuse my product. And it's hard for me to adjust to this stage. I wish I could change the way I see things; I know I have tried. "

Eventually, Frank decided the sales weren't for him, and come to think of it, I should agree with him.
Now, I'm not telling you this story to convince you that you should get out of sales if you don't like rejection. No one likes rejection, and it's natural to feel some disappointment when you hear someone say "no."

But the crucial question is how to deal with this rejection. If you can teach yourself to accept that the fact that the person says "no" is not a reflection on you, your product, or your business, but simply the course of things, you can dust yourself off and move on to the following perspective.

But if you cannot teach yourself this over time, then a career in sales is going to be very difficult for you. Chances are, you'll even start to take the stress out of prospects who don't intend to reject you. If this happens regularly, you have very little chance of success.

Unfortunately, not everyone is suited for a career in sales. Some people, like Frank, have simply invested so much in other ways of working that a change is not a realistic option. For others, luckily, it is possible to capture the resilience and self-confidence necessary to approach the issue of rejection from a detached and professional perspective.

May you feel it now or not, the biggest obstacle to approaching the rejection question is not how the prospect thinks of you but how you think of yourself. Don't be too hard on yourself; Accept steady progress with happiness. If you can make the necessary adjustments and not accept the rejection personally, you will be on your way to sales success.

Don't take responsibility

This chapter may sound like a direct contradiction to the last one, but as you will see, it is not. Taking personal responsibility is a proven method of getting your prospect to pass on important information.

An excellent salesperson I'll call Joe works for a large security guard company in the Midwest. Joe is seventy-two and has been with this company since 1964. If you ask Joe to tell you about his business, he will say to you all sincerity and pride that he works for the number one security company. In the United States of America, without exception.

When Joe is on a sales visit, and he gets to the closing stage of his meeting, he will ask his prospect when would be the best time for the security service to start. Two things can happen. The opportunity can be receptive, in which case Joe will take all the relevant information on a form and set a start date for the service. And, of course, the prospect can step back and say no. This is when something exciting happens.

If the prospect says no, Joe is shocked and somewhat taken aback. It is not an act; he believes so much in his business and ends up knowing so much about his prospect by the time he purchases that he is legitimately worried if he hears an adverse decision.

This is what Joe says: "Mr. Smith, I don't know what to say. I'm so confident that we have the best service, the best prices, the best site customization, and the best reputation of any security guard service in the country that I can only think of one reason you can't. You do not connect with us. And it is that I must have done something wrong earlier in making my presentation to you. I'm going to ask you to help me, Mr. Smith, and show me where I've gone because, to tell you the truth, I know this service is for you, and I would hate to have done them wrong. things are happening. "

What do you think the prospect is saying?

It's pretty hard to come back with your standard response, "Gee, Joe, this just isn't good for us" after all of that, isn't it? If you are Mr. Smith, you probably have a lot of respect for Joe for believing firmly in what he does and for putting himself on the line that way. So, you're not going to mumble something vague and unnecessary from Joe. You are going to give him what he needs - information on where there is a problem.

Typically, what Joe hears at this point is, "No, no, no, it's not you, Joe, it's nothing you've done." It's on our side. "And the prospect will go into detail about the remaining obstacles. Then Joe has the information he needs to continue working with the opportunity.

Suppose I don't have to tell you that Joe is the top-performing salesperson in this organization. By putting aside, the idea that he should always be seen to have done the "right" thing, Joe achieves important goals: he opens up perspective, sheds light on remaining issues, and begins working to resolve them.

You can do the same thing.

Do not show a competitive spirit

In my opinion, if you are a salesman, you are a member of an army, and your army is at war. Fortunately, this type of war has a significant advantage over the standard variety: no one dies in it. But this fact does not diminish by a millimeter the importance of a winning spirit oriented towards competition, nor does it decrease your need and your business for sound battlefield strategies and tactics.

Too many salespeople see themselves as loners, alone. Your business has made a considerable investment in you and will succeed or fail on the battlefield, to a large extent, depending on your performance and that of your colleagues. You share a common goal with many others: the success of your business. To the extent that your business is successful, you will be successful; to the time that your business fails, you will fail.

You're not alone. You are on the front lines, you fight for the customers, and the fight is serious. If you or your business don't take it seriously, you'll lose customers to your competition and eventually "die" - that is, go bankrupt.

You have to be dedicated to winning to gain and keep happy customers because almost certainly someone else wants those customers as badly as you do. That someone will fight for your business and fight to decrease your success as a salesperson in your industry. You have to act aggressively to prevent this from happening.

People often accuse me of being too dramatic when I make this point, but every time they do it, I just tell them that if being too dramatic works for the Chinese, it might help us too. These are the principles by which the Chinese have guided their industries to such fantastic success - and the Japanese before them.

How do you develop a competitive spirit? There are several ways.

Keep an ear open for insight into your business competitors. You talk to customers all day; Find out what your competitors are doing and, just as important, what they are saying about you. Convey the fundamental facts to your "commander."

Report problems to supervisors immediately. If you learn that a customer issue with your product or service seems severe enough to warrant thinking, don't keep it to yourself. Say the "brass" so something can be done immediately.

Develop a team mindset. Know that the other members of your business - administrators, production managers, and other sales department members - all work towards the same goal as you: to be successful for the company. Avoid unnecessary conflicts with your colleagues. Share crucial information that will help your business to emerge. Emphasize positive and optimistic thinking at work.

Set goals for yourself and do all you can to achieve them. Think of your daily schedule as a battle plan, and then put all of your effort into the goals you set for yourself. Don't let complacency or acceptance of mediocrity take hold.

Several companies in this country are already working according to the principles stated above; at the same time, many other companies have institutionalized certain work habits that would not work in an actual combat unit. These are the companies that have good lines of communication, clearly stated goals, and a deep commitment to achieving the results that will flourish in the years to come - and their salespeople will be leading the parade.

Suppose you are working in such a company, congratulations. If you can work to change your business to meet these standards, do it by all means. If you can't fight in the army you currently serve in, find another army - give it all you have.

Good luck!

We are not getting enough information

One of the most vital matters of selling is getting the correct information. People sometimes downplay this side of the process. But, by my calculations, 90% of sales are lost because the representative received incorrect or insufficient information or misinterpreted the information he received.

It seems essential to me that after all these years of teaching, I'm still surprised when students walk into a classroom thinking that information about the product or service they are selling is more important than knowledge. They need to accumulate on the customer. You should know your product inside and out. But knowing how the prospect can use your product is much more critical.

And to understand that, you need to understand the business and how it works, find out what the people who use the product do with it, what the person who buys the product expects from suppliers, and how the business operates. And you need to know all of this before you can make a recommendation. Next, you need to show how using your product or service will help the business do what it does now - better and more profitably.

How do you get the kind of information you need? The first and vital common way is to ask questions. The apparent wisdom is that you are supposed to ask "open-ended" questions, that is, questions that cannot be answered with either a "yes" or a "no." That's right, but it's much more complicated than that.

Neither you nor the prospect wants to sit there listening to you ask and answer a long list of questions. What you want is a give-and-take conversation between the two of you and generate the responses you need.

Not only does this provide information, but engaging the prospect in a conversation involves them in your efforts. The exchange of discussions makes perspective more than a source of animated information; he becomes an active participant in your sales process.

How do you start a conversation? If you are in sales and don't know how to have a conversation, let me respectfully suggest that you have made a poor career choice. You start a conversation with a prospect like you start a conversation with a stranger at a party. "Hi, what are you doing? How long have you been doing this? What were you doing before?"

But getting enough information from a prospect - say, a purchasing manager - is only enough if he or she is the only one making the buying decision. In this case, inputs from other sources are less necessary. But if, for example, you are selling something that goes through a thorough review process with a final decision made by a committee, you must use more than one source of information.

It's like witnessing an accident. No one seems to see what happened the same way. This also happens in sales. Some will see your product from a cost perspective. Others will see it from an ease-of-use angle. That's why I always try to speak to as many people as possible to give myself a better idea of the whole picture - from all angles.

I call it the power of twelve. When I sell to a large corporation, I try to hit the grassroots with at least a dozen people at all levels of the hierarchy. I speak to company field sales reps, telemarketers, customer service people, sales managers, sales leads, and vice presidents. I want to know more about the company than most executives because the more I know, the better I am to develop a training solution for what ails them.

This should also be your goal. If possible, talk to people in the manufacturing industry to see if there are any issues with the product they are currently using, talk to salespeople and see what complaints, if any, they receive from customers, talk to managers of sales for ideas they might have that might make their product more attractive.

Not only do you learn something from everyone you talk to who can help your cause, but every conversation allows you to appeal to another ally. If someone is unhappy with the cost of the current provider's widgets, and you can show them how much money they're going to save, that person becomes an ally. If someone is worried about the quality and you can assure them of the superiority of your product, well, you've got another partner.

In short, you can never have enough information - just like you can never have enough commissions. Coincidence?

It does not know when to stop talking
Years ago, I saw a poster in my insurance agent's office that I found extremely rude - at first. It said:

Implement
• Configure

- Put it down
- And shut up

But the more I thought about that day later, the more I came to recognize the wisdom of those words, especially when it came to sales. It's impossible to quantify, but I'm convinced that a decent percentage of sales are lost because reps just don't know when to stop talking.

There are two schools of sales protocol. It is said that sales are made and lost in the presentation - that is, in words, brought to the table by the sales rep. The other thinks that the sales rep's job is not to speak but to listen to what the prospect says.

As always, the reply lies somewhere in between. Obviously, as I note in error 28: Not getting enough information, the sales rep has to talk, and just as obviously, the sales rep has to listen. But it doesn't always happen in the proper proportions.

Most often, the problem is associated with the sales representative's ego. We've all met the rep who thinks he knows everything - and isn't shy about letting everyone around him know how smart he is. Suppose for a moment that you are an expert on your product. You know how it's made. You know how it can be used. You know how it should be sold.

What if someone walks in and tells you that everything you know is entirely wrong, that they know the absolute truth, and that you should be grateful that they want to share it with you? What do you think you would say to him? Do the words "shut up" come to mind?

Let's say someone walks in and spends most of their time in the meeting talking about their exploits - how many widgets they've sold, how many companies they work with, all the places their devices are used - without a word on how you might use them. What could be your reaction? Do the terms "shut up" come to mind?

Or how about a sales rep who asks appropriate questions but doesn't bother to listen to your answers. As a result, his proposal is entirely irrelevant. What could be your reaction? Do the words "shut up" come to mind?

It's not like I don't sometimes feel the urge to chat; we all do. But the guide I use is to ask myself how I would think if I was the recipient of this conversation. Would I want me to stop? Is it that I feel enough said?

I also have a simple "know when to stop talking" plan. Before I go to a meeting, I write down what I want to accomplish. Maybe it's just to get some questions answered. Perhaps it will be to see if I can get an agreement to meet other people in the company. Maybe this is to be "straightened out" - that is, to see if the information I have received to date - and my interpretation - is correct. Once I hit my goal (and set the next step in place), I get out of there as fast as I can politely.

"Fish and visitors smell in three days." Steve Schiffman says, "Nothing can poison a business faster than a sales rep who doesn't know when to stop talking."

The rule of closure is even more important when presenting. You come up with your proposal, repeat the accent points, then remain silent. You can ask if there are any questions, points that need clarification or even request an order.

But don't repeat yourself. Very few things are worse than a salesperson buzzing over and over, repeating points like prospects are fools and didn't get the moment the first four times he brought them up.

Silence can be an essential weapon in your arsenal. It's okay to let the prospect fill the void.
The bottom line is that if your message is relevant and delivered correctly, the prospect will get it. If not, no matter how much you talk, you will not overcome this error.

And on the subject of mistakes, let me tell you a sadly true story. I had landed a sale (in my mind, anyway), said goodbye and leaving, asked if I could use the phone. The prospect said yes, and while I was dialing, they picked up a book and asked me what I thought.

I reacted negatively, only to find out that he wrote one of the sections of the book. When I finished the call, the prospect said, "We might have to rethink this." I lost the sale. If only I had followed my advice and walked out of there without saying a word...
Remember to do what I say, not what I do.

Chapter # 8

20 things you should do (and not do) to make a sale

The whole sales process can be long and tortuous, but with the right strategy, you can reduce purchase friction significantly; we tell you how.

Making a sale can be annoying and challenging, but knowing the dos and don'ts for every presentation should make it easier for you to close deals.

We consulted sales coach and writer Wendy Weiss (also known as the Queen of Cold), Jill Konrath, author of "SNAP Buying and Selling Big Companies," and Paul, Jedi Mastery, Vice President of Castin Training Systems Castain compiles the following two lists: 10 things that salespeople should never do, and ten things that salespeople should never do.

Here are the ten things' salespeople should never do:

1. Never show poor etiquette in person or over the phone.
Weiss says chewing gum, eating, having music or the television blasting in the background, talking to other people while on the phone, being late, murmuring, or not speaking are leading causes of customer churn and are attitudes. Just rude. Any of these things can significantly reduce your chances of making the sale.

Konrath says looking at your phone during a meeting is another major insult. Use common sense and treat your buyer with respect.

2. Never jump to conclusions in advance or try to read their minds.
"The prospect is in a meeting" doesn't necessarily mean that "The prospect knows you're calling and doesn't want to talk to you," Weiss says. "I'm busy I can't talk right now" doesn't translate to "I don't want to talk to you, and I'm not interested," he adds. "Too many salespeople read negatively the statements made by their potential clients."

3. Never be negative.
Don't let failure enter your vocabulary, says Konrath. "Redefine everything as learning, and then focus on how to get different results."

4. Never discuss something inappropriate.
Never discuss politics with a prospect or customer unless you are 100% sure they share the opinion, Konrath suggests. "And yet, it may not be a good decision because other members of the decision-making team may have different opinions."

Sellers can ask questions but cannot cross the line. It is good to know your potential client. However, it would be best if you never asked too many personal questions, or that may make them feel uncomfortable.

5. Never pretend to know the answer to something when it is not.
There is absolutely nothing shameful about telling someone you don't know the answer to something but that you will find out and let them

know as soon as possible. "It never happened to me that I admit not having the answer to a question and that the client has said to me, 'How dare you?' Usually, the client will appreciate your honesty. And if it doesn't, it's a good indicator that it's not a good option," says Captain.

6. Never rely on the phone as your only source of lead generation.
Everyone has their favourite means of communication, so be sure to use a well-balanced mix of phone, email, social media, mainstream networking, and other creative approaches. Otherwise, you'll limit your results, Castain recommends.

7. Never ask stupid questions.
It would help if you asked questions, but not about anything you can easily find on a business website. "You're going to lose credibility if you do it," Konrath warns.

8. Never be defensive.
Some sellers feel the need to defend them (or are ashamed of them), but that could be a red flag for the prospect, says Captain. If the price is higher than what the potential customer wants, remind them of the value and benefits.

9. Never get too comfortable.
You should never stop looking for prospects, even if you have confidence in your customer base. "You should always concentrate on bringing in new businesses, securing existing ones, and growing them

and growing," says Captain. "Always keep a good balance in those things and never feel too comfortable."

10. Never improvise.
See number 2 on the "must-do" list.

Now, here are the top 10 recommendations from the experts on the things you should always do:

1. Always segment your prospects well.
Too many sales professionals spend too much time chasing inappropriate prospects. "Sales reps can take advantage of their time doing their homework and reaching out to only the right prospects," says Weiss.

2. Always be prepared.
"Leading sales professionals DO NOT improvise. They make it look simple, and that's because they are prepared," says Weiss.

Do a quick search for your prospect, check their website, or look them up on a site like LinkedIn before their first meeting. "What you discover can provide you with good tools to create a connection," says Konrath.

3. Always ask questions.
"Try always to ask the questions that make your customers think," says Captain. "A better question might get you an answer, but a great question raises the person inside your prospect, who could be where your biggest competitor lives."

4. Always listen.

Too many sales reps talk too much. Weiss suggests following the 80/20 rule. "The rep should spend 20% of the time talking and 80% of the time listening to their prospect," he recommends.

5. Always adds value.

Concentrate on the difference you can make, not how you are different from your competition, says Konrath. "Your prospects need you to convey the value you offer to their business to determine if the change in the status quo makes sense."

6. Always focus on solutions.

It would help if you always thought about how you can help your prospect fix a problem they have, says Captain. "Besides concentrating on solutions for your business, too. If you are having trouble with a particular sale, think about how you can approach it in another way. "

7. Always get at the point of yourself in the shoes of your prospects.

Always stay in a frame of mind where you can think about things from your client's perspective, says Captain. "If you were him, what would your most significant challenges be? What are your most enormous opportunities? Once you have this level of awareness, focus all your artillery on being helpful. "

8. Always be honest.

Be honest about prices and additional fees the customer may incur, says Captain. Also, always be truthful with bad news. Give your clients the information ahead of time. The sooner you do it, the more options will be available".

9. Always ask for what you want.
"The biggest reason salespeople aren't able to schedule appointments or close sales is that they don't ask for the appointment or don't ask to close the sale," says Weiss. Share your intentions with your prospect.

10. Always follow up.
"In today's crowded market, prospects have forgotten about almost all follow-up activities," says Konrath. Call or email shortly after the meeting or conversation to stay on the prospect's mind.

Then follow up on yourself. "Always evaluate yourself after a sales meeting," adds Konrath. "Look at what you've done well so that you can repeat it, and identify your obstacles so that you can develop ways to avoid them in the future."

Chapter # 9

The 3 "traps" (and more) of salespeople who almost always sell

90% of commercial visits end without a sale. However, there are some sellers, very few, the good ones, who can sell almost always.

How do they do that? What do good salespeople do to increase their business effectiveness ratio?
To sell more you need, first of all, a proper arrangement. Selling is an attitude of mind.
And secondly, technique.

With the right mindset and mastery of technique, nothing stops a salesperson from becoming a better salesperson.

But what else does it take to sell most of the time?
To sell, you almost always have to do some "tricks." Namely:

1.- If the commercial ratio is measured as No. of sales / No. of visits, the good salesperson knows that to increase the commercial ratio, it is necessary to "reduce" the number of visits. Therefore, the excellent salesman works before he sells. You spend time studying your prospects to avoid gambling. He only acts when he knows there are possibilities. That is, choose well. Choose. If you try to sell to anyone, you are simply overworking. You will be making sterile visits that only serve to stain your CV by lowering your commercial ratio.

2.- Good salespeople don't work for just any company. They choose the company they work for very well. They know that with a good product, the closing ratio increases.

3.- Good salespeople, those who have the right mental attitude and use the technique, also demand to have the best price. They make sure that no one will be in a position to offer something similar for a lower price.

Mental attitude, technique, cheating, and... something else?

Sure. A good salesperson knows that any closing, to conclude successfully, requires proof of results. Ultimately, all favourable business negotiations end with a precise **"Profitability Analysis. "**

To increase your sales, don't leave your sales team unattended. Motivate them, teach them effective business techniques, share the strategies of the no-failures, and turn them into advanced salespeople.

Chapter # 10

The Best Practices for Increasing Sales

The eight best practices to increase sales
Do you want to increase your turnover?

Whether for products, services, or an idea, the foundation of a business rests on the ability to sell because, as the saying goes: "A man full of ideas which do not know how to sell them will not go." further than a man without ideas."

Are you a CEO, wants to know what your sales team should be doing to finally get the numbers off the ground or outperform the market?

Are you a sales manager? Do you want to know what to expect from your teams?
Are you a salesperson? Do you want to know what remains to be done to make a better living?
Find below some common-sense practices that are fundamental to your success.

1 - Always prospect regularly

Not prospecting regularly exposes you to a lack of opportunities 1 to 2 or 6 months later, and therefore there will inevitably be a hole in your business. Companies face inconsistent results because they tolerate inconsistency in supplying the pipeline.

Prospecting must become a NON-REPORTABLE meeting with yourself and your future clients. During this time, you do nothing other than making phone calls back-to-back. The CRM update is after!

2 - Always ask for references and introductions

When salespeople (managers and presidents are allowed to do this too!) Speak with your prospects and customers; they should always ask for referrals and introductions! Sales growth is closely related to the number of opportunities that enter the pipeline and their quality.

Referrals and introductions generate better conversion ratios compared to all other sources of potential customers. The main reason your salespeople don't get referrals is that they don't ask for them!

Also, remind them that the best way to get some is to donate first.
How to ask for recommendations is here ... but don't forget, no matter how you ask, above all, you have to ASK SYSTEMATICALLY.

3 - Always keep your team accountable

Remember, your role is to keep your sales force accountable to sales growth goals and the plan that has been developed to achieve those goals. The best way to keep your team responsible for the project and what activities everyone needs to do is to meet daily.

A 5–7-minute meeting each morning will keep the team focused on what they need to accomplish. This will quickly expose any gap between expectations and what happened.

4 - Always monitor behaviours and activities

Tracking activities and behaviours are the only natural way to manage sales proactively. By looking at daily and weekly activities and behaviours, you stay on top of upcoming results, and you can put in place an action plan to correct any deviations before it's too late ... which can mean before it's finished off the month or quarter when the quotas must be reached.

It is dangerous to drive a car while looking in the rear-view mirror. It is also challenging to look at an Excel table with € from the past to predict the future ...

5 - Always follow the sales process

Your sales process should be a proven recipe that is repeatable to achieve sales goals. It is only by following the process that you can predictably grow your business.

If you want to increase your income, you will have to be obsessed with having an optimized sales process. It should be designed specifically for your business, market, industry, and product and help your sales force overcome the specific obstacles they will encounter in a sale.

6 - Always be firm on prices

When you are not firm on your prices, you are setting a precedent. You open the door for your salespeople and demonstrate that it's okay to give a potential customer an offer at a lower price to close the sale.

You should also eliminate any exceptions and make sure the pricing isn't too complicated to manage. The job of the sales manager is not to manage price exceptions.

7 - Always Coaching Your Team V enter

You can't build your team and give them ad hoc training. You need to train your team daily. Coaching can be done formally or informally, but in all cases, it must be done daily. There are two types of coaching you should provide to your salespeople: pre-meeting preparation and post-meeting debriefing. What are the skills that build a sales culture?

8 - Never Accept Apologies

They are making excuses often become part of an organization's sales culture despite top management's best efforts. These excuses decrease your sales force's ability to grow sales steadily.

Your sales organization should not only be committed to sales growth goals, but it should also be fully accountable for results!

Before pointing at officials with your index finger, use your thumb, and you will see who it is pointing to ...

If you want to make a clear instinct, Objective Management Group tools and the associated recruiting method will help you make a difference for good. Finally, recruit the best salespeople who will sell!

Do you want to increase your sales potential? Whether it's some digital or physical item, service, or idea, the foundation of a business is the ability to sell. When it comes to selling and closing business, your prospects don't want to be told stories. Having qualities as a salesperson means knowing how to listen attentively, have a critical mind, and apply your sales techniques effectively.

As a CEO, you are aware of the importance of having and building a successful team that will move the company forward for you and know how to apply your business tactics. To do this, your sales force should follow these best practices:

1 - Always prospect regularly
Salespeople shouldn't find themselves running out of sales opportunities for one month and then working harder to make up for it the next month. They must remain regular in prospecting. **Companies face inconsistent results because they tolerate inconsistencies** in exploration and bringing new opportunities into the pipeline.

Advice for sellers:
- Put prospecting slots on your schedule each week AND respect these dedicated times
- Be prepared when you start your prospecting
- Cut yourself off from distractions such as emails

Tips for Sales Managers:

- Make prospecting activities mandatory
- Follow each week the prospecting activities carried out by each salesperson and the results they obtain

2 - Always ask for references and introductions

When reps speak with prospects and clients, they should always ask for referrals and introductions! **Sales growth is closely related to the number of opportunities that enter the pipeline and their quality.**

Referrals and introductions generate better conversion ratios compared to all other sources of potential customers. The leading reason sellers don't get referrals is because they don't ask for them! **Remind them that 80% of introductions lead to sales.**

3 - Always keep an entire pipeline

In connection with the first point, it is essential not to wait until the pipeline of opportunities is empty to prospect. You need to know the average sales cycle length to know when an opportunity that enters the channel should close.

If enough leads are entering the pipeline, sales will naturally follow. It is essential to remain constant. A sawtooth effort will only give you roller-coaster results.

Tips for sellers:
- Make sure to add sales opportunities in sufficient quantity (number of options) and with a good level of quality (value of options)

- Once opportunities enter the pipeline, they must advance to closing by going through the sales process or be disqualified. Simply put, there must be constant movement in the channel.

Tips for Sales Managers:
- Do regular pipeline reviews with each of your reps.
- Make sure the pipeline's weighted value is consistently aligned with sales targets.
- Be firm and disqualify opportunities that appear to be abandoned if the broker defines no next step.
-

4 - Always keep your team accountable

The role of sales managers is to keep the sales force accountable to sales growth goals and the plan that has been developed to achieve those goals. The best way to keep a sales team responsible for the project and the activities each one needs to do is to meet up daily.

A 5–7-minute meeting each morning will keep the team focused on what they need to accomplish. This will quickly expose any gap between expectations and what happened.

5 - Always monitor behaviours and activities

Tracking activities and behaviours are the only natural way to manage sales proactively. By looking at daily and weekly activities and behaviours, you stay **on top of upcoming results. You can put in place an action plan to correct any deviations** before it's too late ... which can mean before the end of the month or quarter when the quotas must be met.

Conversely, results indicators such as turnover or sales profitability make it possible to conclude. While these indicators are critical, they do not allow decisions to be taken early enough to avoid significant deviations between reality and forecasts.

6 - Always follow the sales process

The **sales process should be a proven recipe that is repeatable** to achieve sales goals. It is through repeating this sales process that it is possible to move sales predictably.

To increase sales revenue, you have to work on optimizing the sales process constantly. It should be designed specifically for your business, market, industry, and product and help the sales force overcome specific obstacles they will encounter in a sale.

Today, technology helps optimize sales processes using data entered into CRMs such as Membrane.

7 - Always be firm on prices

When sellers are not firm on price when bidding, it creates a situation where they think they can always get a better price. Sales managers who accept this practice from their salespeople lose critical business markup percentages and show that it's okay to give a potential customer a discount to close the sale.

I have seen companies where sales managers spent more than 50% of their time managing price exceptions given to customers over time.

To increase sales, you need to focus more on value than on price.

8 - Always have the urgency to conclude

Be careful; we must understand the notion of urgency to be concluded. It is not about wanting to "close" clients at all costs during the first meeting or pressure the client. Also, representatives can interpret a request for quotation to signify that the customer is ready to sign when he wants information from the seller.

Representatives should have a sense of urgency to close when all stages of the sales process are completed, and the customer needs to make a buying decision.

9 - Always coach your sales team

Coaching representatives is the number one priority of the most effective sales managers. They spend at least 50% of their time coaching.

Often, coaching is seen as a very different task than it is!

Coaching can be done formally or informally, but in all cases, it must be done daily. To start coaching representatives individually, you need to focus on two activities: **pre-meeting preparation and post-meeting debriefing.**

10 - Never accept excuses

They are making excuses often become part of an organization's sales culture despite top management's best efforts. These excuses diminish the ability of the sales force to grow its sales steadily.

There will never be an ideal situation in which representatives can achieve all of the goals. Therefore, sales forces must contend with fluctuations in the economy, aggressive competition, the company's selling prices, and other factors. These are things over which representatives and sales managers do not have direct control, so they are the most common excuses given to explain the lack of performance.

Sales managers, therefore, have an essential job to do to fight against excuses and help reps work on factors they control, such as their prospecting and sales activities or even respecting the sales process.

To remember:

To succeed in increasing sales regardless of the context, sales forces, including leaders, need to structure themselves, follow the best practices listed above, and be constant in efforts and improvement.

Chapter # 11

How to be good at your job?

The two sales performance experts discussed how to recognize a good salesperson, particularly the eight strategies to become an exceptional salesperson FINALLY. According to the specialist, it is essential to train like a top athlete and bring together particular qualities ...

Curiosity: quality number 1 According to Evelyne Platonic Cohen, the first quality that we must find in an exceptional salesperson is curiosity: *"There are those who know Everything and those who are aware of not knowing Everything but who do not seek to show interest. "* There remains a minority of people who believe that there is a lot to learn to gain skills. This is an essential quality that we see in elite salespeople. It is, above all, a character trait that can be educated.

In a skillful world, you always have to know more than your competitor to differentiate yourself. During the interview, we identify this type of profile about the questions asked by the candidate, if he is more interested in the functioning of the company and does not focus only on salary advantages ... Thus, the recruiter can analyze the depth and relevance in the candidate's search for information, a good indicator of curiosity!

Tenacity and organization, the perfect combo

When we study the skills required of a salesperson, we spontaneously imagine a determined person who does not give up easily. Tenacity is the will never to let go, a character trait that is highly sought after in the sales function. For the expert, this quality must be accompanied by a strict organization. To revive and follow its customers, the organization of the sales representative is essential since these are very technical stages. It is also the intelligence to maintain a good relationship with its customer and create a guideline of actions that must apply to a salesperson.

We analyze the tenacity level by asking him: how is he organized to follow a client to the end? Based on his answers, we can quickly see his ability to plan his tasks.

Creativity: a decisive skill that distinguishes a good salesperson and an exceptional salesperson
The main difference between these two profiles is the dose of creativity. Unfortunately, this is not something that can be learned or worked on. It's an integral part of a salesperson's personality. The Founder of Booster Academy defines creativity as *"the ability to have an argument based on the needs of her client."* An exceptional salesperson can quickly adapt his speech and his demonstration according to his interlocutor.

Even with a lack of creativity, the salesperson can do it differently and as intelligently. So, it's not a tragedy! To compensate for this deficiency of creativity, the salesperson's presentation support can help bring richness and relevance to the salesperson's pitch. The Touch & Sell solution enables it possible to do this since the salesperson has an application in his company's colours, within which gathers all the documents he needs to sell his product and service.

Preparation: an exceptional art
Obviously, and we do not teach you anything, it takes good preparation before your meeting to gain in sales performance at the point of contact. Practice includes a seller's knowledge of their ecosystem, market, and competitors. For Evelyne Platonic Cohen: *"I don't see how a salesperson can wake up without listening to BFM Business. I know you want to listen to music, but that's not what will increase your sales".*

At the same time, there is all the knowledge of the customer, which is essential. In recent years, a salesperson has had more elements at his fingertips. He can "track" his interlocutor, which significantly facilitates his work. The sales expert explains, *"Not everything you know about your client should always be used."* At what rhyme all this investigation in this case? You must know how to use it at the right time and not unpack Everything to the interlocutor unless you want to scare him... This knowledge is to be used subtly! For example, if the client is a football fan, comparing the service offering to the world of sport or telling anecdotes related to this theme work in the salesperson's favour.

Anticipation: adapt to each scenario
The Founder of Booster Academy explains that selling is like a game of chess. To best anticipate a business meeting, the seller must know all the

combinations that make up this point of contact. Evelyne Platonic Cohen gives the example of a great chess player.

He spent his time learning and understanding the old strategies put in place by other players. According to her: *"You always have to ask yourself; how can I be better and what is my tactic to achieve my goal? "*. You have to stay in a constant dynamic of learning and keep in mind the desire to be better and surpass yourself.

The vision: to project oneself to evolve better
"The salespeople who have a vision of their job are those who will manage to evolve in their hierarchy," according to the expert. When a salesperson leaves his client's home, he must be able to know whether he won the contract or not, even if the meeting went wrong. There are no miracle tricks to have 100% closing, just well-established sales techniques.

The culture of "winning": 100% commercial
It is a characteristic specific to the best salespeople who always want more and do not settle for the minimum. You have to love success and victories to create a virtuous circle of enthusiasm and resilience in the face of obstacles. For the Foundress, there is no formation to obtain the culture of winning. You have to look at its history and past to understand where this deep determination comes from.

Letting go: the work of a lifetime

The last secret of the exceptional commercial is no less essential: to let go. Indeed, knowing how to let go in a meeting allows you to be turned entirely towards your interlocutor, to listen fully without prejudice or expectation of result. This behaviour makes the discussion more natural and creates a climate of trust with the person while remaining detached.

Conclusion

Working on each of the qualities listed and dedicated to the exceptional salesperson will allow salespeople to climb the ladder more quickly! However, one essential point for Guillaume Legendre, COO at Touch & Sell, is missing to excel in this profession. He is talking about the business presentation medium, the excellent seller's briefcase.

We first think that a good salesperson can sell anything, anywhere and therefore does not need any content to achieve his goal… This is not quite the case … To develop its effectiveness in meetings, the salesperson needs innovative means and tools. The Company Manager recommends equipping sales representatives with touchscreen tablets that contribute to the development of the customer experience and its performance!

Chapter # 12

The commandments of a good salesperson!

Every salesperson's dream is to be a good salesperson!
He is the person who brought back the contract with a shovel, exceeded the sales target, effectively opened up the prospects, and achieved the best turnover... Everything is in order!

Being a good salesperson or a good salesperson means:

But how do you go about becoming the great salesperson that every business is snapping up? You think it's not within your reach. Think again! Follow these ten commandments: you too will become a Super Commercial, and you will be the pet peeve of the competition!
A lousy salesperson can be deceived, but not for long: if he gets good results, it never lasts!

A good, even a very good, salesperson is characterized by elements that do not deceive:

- It meets and exceeds the objectives.

- He reproduces his performances systematically and regularly.
- Its results are always just as good, whatever the economic situation, competitive rivalries, and external and internal risks.

For what reason? He produced his own sales technique, mastered it perfectly, and adopted a unified and attractive business attitude: he knows how to speak in the ears of customers/prospects!

Becoming a successful and efficient salesperson is neither reserved for an elite nor innate. It's good news! You can achieve this Holy Grail as long as you follow these ten pro tips and tricks.

Did you know? Evelyne Platonic-Cohen, the founder of the Booster Academy, has created an intensive sales training center. A proper reference in her field is living proof that any salesperson can become an exceptional salesperson if he follows the correct principles and applies them!

Introduce yourself effectively and make you want to build customer relationships

Sell yourself before you even try to sell the product/service to the customer! Knowing how to present yourself in the shortest possible time is essential to attract interlocutors and get their attention.

In just a few minutes (because the customer's time is as precious as yours), to show you a complex business proposal.

Make your interlocutor want to build a customer relationship with you. Adapt your introduction to customers/prospects to get their support. The reassuring speech inspired her confidence. Your interlocutor said to himself when listening to you: "I have a good feeling for this salesman. He understands me and knows how to talk to me."

You will work with a real team of potential clients/client leaders and let him wish to be a part of it!

Practice active listening to get a personalized response
Have you dealt with this sales representative, and he recites his views in the field of automation without listening to your comments? Not the most effective way to complete the sale!
Forget the standardized speech! If you pitch a pitch without considering the real needs of your customers to sell your products at all costs, failure is guaranteed!

During the discovery phase, practice active listening:
- Let your client/prospect do the talking.
- Ask him good questions (open and closed) to identify his motivations, possible obstacles, and real needs.
- Facilitate interactions between you and your interlocutor to create a bond.
- Tailor your answer or solution precisely.

Far from being an unproductive commercial monologue, this constructive exchange allows you to propose an offer adapted to the context, the sector, the customer, and problems.

Openly demonstrate your empathy and interest. Your interlocutor will be sensitive to it! He will say to himself: "This salesperson listened to me, understood me, and offered me the best solution." How to resist?

Working on customer relations is a competitive advantage. Put the buyer at the core of your concerns, and you will get their preference!

Be an honest seller.

Some salespeople are tempted to embellish reality to gain leads. This is a rookie mistake!
If you lie to a customer, they won't get caught twice. Worse, it risks giving you a terrible reputation in the industry!

Do not commit to deadlines if you cannot meet them, nor to the technical performance of your products if they do not correspond to reality. Likewise, don't sell a solution that doesn't match your customer (to make the numbers).

To retain your customers, respect your commitments! Maintaining a relationship of truth with a buyer is the key to working with them long-term and attracting others through word of mouth.

Master sales techniques
You do not become a successful sales agent without rigorous training. Having a flair is not enough to be one of the best sellers!

The trade of salesperson cannot be improvised. Learn all the techniques to use during the sales process:
- Prospecting: ABM, CAB, BEBEDC ...
- Argumentation
- Negotiation: SPANCO, 4C, CAP SONCAS ...
- Closing: BATNA / MORE, SNAP Selling, SIMAC ...

Do these acronyms mean nothing to you? Take stock of the 12 bestselling techniques.

And it is not enough to know them in theory! Work on sales techniques to master them perfectly in practice and make them your own. **Your client will not even realize that he is moving from the discovery phase to the closing phase**!

Do you master them? So much the better! But the goal is not to stupidly bring out all these methods during a sales interview! Draw the one that best suits the situation and the prospect/customer.

Good to know: the sequence between the different stages of sale must be fluid. Practice moving from sales argumentation to negotiation to end up closing as naturally as possible!

Promote your commercial expertise

Commercial expertise is one of the qualities that a top seller must cultivate.

When customers/prospects find information on Google by themselves, they stand out by bringing them real added value.

Improve a customer's shopping experience thanks to your expertise on:
- your sector
- your business and hers
- your product/service offers
- technological, technical, organizational, HR innovations, etc.
- New regulations.

The customer must be convinced: without you, he would make the wrong choice!

1. Bet on customer satisfaction and feelings

A client will be ready to pay the price, whatever it is, if he is convinced that his investment will be profitable thanks to:

- **To your commercial expert advice.** Support him with a relevant consultancy service until the appropriate solution is found.
- **To the ultra-competitive advantages of your products/services** which perfectly meet its needs.

Do not miss the feeling and customer satisfaction! Show your interlocutor that the benefits of your offer and your expertise are worth their investment.

"Loyal customers don't just come back to you; they don't just recommend you; they insist their friends do business with you."
Chip Bell

Empower yourself to be the best seller

The mind of a salesperson is one of the keys to success. Do you want to succeed? You will succeed! But you still have to work, work and not hesitate to... work!

To perform and remain so, willpower is a professional engine that other qualities must accompany:
- Be convinced that you are the best to convince your customer in turn! Be determined to succeed: you will gain thickness in front of your interlocutor. You will impose, and your proposal will gain credibility.
- Question yourself if specific methods don't work. Learn from your mistakes. Remember: it's only morons who don't change their minds.
- Do not stay on your own. Take regular training courses to be on top of the latest sales techniques that work!
- Make the sales practices your own: test them in the field repeatedly with your customers until you find your own sales generators!

Progress through training
Whether you are a young, newbie salesperson or an oldie, don't think you have anything more to learn. If you wish to be an effective salesperson, there is only one solution: training!

Get trained:
- new business methods such as social selling (prospecting and sales via social networks).

- In personal development to gain self-confidence in the field.
- Thanks to innovative team-building activities using technology to stimulate your desire to perform and take advantage of the group dynamic.

Please do not sleep on your laurels; they may dry out! Be active in the evolution of your trade. To progress, you have to train continuously!

Embrace situational business intelligence
Don't just use the sales tools without showing a minimum of intelligence! Instead, practice situational business intelligence; that is to say? Use a sales pitch adapted at the right time with the right interlocutor according to the context.

You precisely target the sales method and response according to the needs of your client/prospect. The result? Your interlocutor is won over! Because you make him a relevant and personalized offer with a memorable speech.

Optimize your sales process through sales talks
To gain in performance, have you already tried the PDCA method?

Whatever the field, this technique, also called the Deming Wheel, works wonders to boost your business results continuously.
Improve your process in 4 steps:

- **Plan: plan!** Establish a business plan of action to leave no room for improvisation. Sales interviews, commercial activities, sales pitch, handling of objections ... Everything must be considered, prepared, and anticipated.
- **Do: apply and test!** Develop your sales plan during customer interviews according to the recommended actions.
- **Check: check!** Check the results obtained. Take a clear picture: which business goals are being achieved and which need to be improved. Use the means of control at your disposal (commercial performance indicators) to analyze what is working ... or not!
- **Act: adjust and act!** No need to wait for the outcomes to come back by themselves! Correct the situation immediately with adapted solutions and use your new commercial action plan from the next meetings.

With this method, you are sure to progress through each sales cycle, as long as you plan, test, verify and adjust, then act systematically!

Chapter # 13

Habits of incredibly successful salespeople

How to make a good sales staff

The difference between a better salesperson and a good salesperson is fantastic. Good sales representatives reach their quota most of the time. Excellent sales representatives not only continued to be hit attack but also leave a few months or quarters. Exceptional sales representatives have won the trust and respect of potential customers.

Excellent sales representatives have won the appreciation, loyalty, and recommendation of potential customers. Good representatives can handle objections proficiently. Great sales representatives will preemptively eliminate these worries and make them disappear.

If you want to be great, that is good news. Following these rules of a good seller will help you become one of the best-selling salespeople in your team and even your company.

Identify and adhere to your buyer angle colour
Ming determines to mean the buyer's role is essential for an effective sales process. Sales representatives who insist on this role can effectively generate sales. Otherwise, the salesperson may be the next best thing to use spray strategy, resulting in low exploration efficiency.

Adequate research on behalf of the prospects will be to ensure he was very appropriate. They insist on their ideal buyer role and know exactly who they want to sell to and why.

Use measurable, re-double the sales flow processes
The table now poor representatives' intuition to guide them. Efficient sales representatives using optimized processes can be as many potential customers from the "connection" transferred to "shut closed. "

The table now represents the poor always let things slip through the cracks. Efficient sales representatives know each transaction's status in their pipeline, what actions they will take next, and when they will be executed. Poor-performing sales representatives never result - because as they do not track the results. High-performance sales representatives will obsessively review their key indicators and make adjustments as needed.

TL; DR: It's extraordinary; you need a consistent process.

Understand your yield product

Can be enough to sell is half the battle. The other half (usually undervalued) is the way to understand what you are selling.

In the past, sales relied on charm and snake oil tactics. However, now, potential customers have more access to information than ever before, so they are not easy to fool. To attain their trust and add value to their lives, you must truly understand your product.

Off concept review your tube channel

Influential sales representatives will not mark transactions as possible because of influencers like them. He was able to objectively review their opportunities and avoid happiness and make accurate sales forecasts.

Find shortcuts and black passengers

Excellent after-sales staff to find a viable strategy or technology will use it repeatedly until it stops working so far.

This is very clever. Representatives are always working non-stop, which means they spend more time experimenting, and they have less time to make sales. In addition, there is an opportunity cost. Trying one thing doesn't work, but you miss the opportunity to use a proven option.

I'm not built recommends that you do not change his approach. Just do this selectively and get results as quickly as possible to implement the strategy or move on.

Exercise initiative, hear, listen.
Successful when the sales staff to communicate with potential customers, they will be kept entirely in. He had not considered other deals, browse Reddit thread or send a funny meme to team members. They got engaged - therefore, he had more in-depth dialogue with buyers and meaningful.

The main action might be to listen to one of the most challenging skills developments because human nature is, compared to the potential customers, that you care more about what you want to say. However, it is precious. Not only can you build stronger relationships, but you can also unlock information, which will help you position your product as the best option.

Efforts to work for
5 pm on the last day of the month or quarter. B-ball member has left office - he had at a nearby bar to celebrate because they have reached the quota. C player still in office - he is sending an email last attempt to show potential customers a few weeks has not been used. A ball member is also in the office. They have succeeded, but they are still sending emails, arranging meetings, and making phone calls. By establishing the foundation for the month, they need, they always leave the goal behind.

With feed

After sending the proposal, many sales staff failed to follow up effectively. They don't even know if potential customers have opened their emails.

HubSpot Sales can help solve this problem by letting salespeople know when and how often a potential customer opens an email. With this data, they can follow up at the best time.

Personalize your letter of interest

High-performing salespeople do not follow the script and treat each potential customer in a "one size fits all" approach. Still, they are committed to learning as much information about potential customers as possible to tailor their information. These sales representatives understand their customers' unique pain points and explain why their products are very suitable.

Shield your same age people

Do you want to improve your exclusive meetings deal with? Verify that your company had been masters of long sales staff and ask if you can cover some of their phones. Learning from great instructors is a great way to improve your work while building strong relationships with colleagues.

Practice your interpersonal communication can force

Excellent chat is a Zhong learned skill - which pushes critical to the success of the salesman. Whether you are having a housewarming party or participating in a social event, you should practice making others feel at ease. Please pay attention to what makes them open, zoning and laughter, and then take what you learned back to the office.

As for the team's
So much sales pop culture beautifies the lone wolf in sales. But the best salespeople know, something to build industry and successful sales team takes a village. Help your fellows know when to ask for help - this is the key to a long and fulfilling sales career.

What to know what time to go to open
If you are in the waves, fee alone is not a lot of time to carry out a transaction? Know what your average transaction time is, and use it to guide how long it takes to buy a transaction. There are exceptions to this rule. However, if your average sales cycle is 45 days and your marketing is 90 days old, please consider using Sandler to correct this method's results.

He says actual words.
Tell customers what you want to close the day is over. Don't promise features that don't exist yet, prices that cannot be offered, or the company's inability to provide outstanding services. This may make you a successful business, but it will not be able to maintain its business. In the end, you will get bad reviews and a bad reputation. In addition, new research shows that honesty can help you live a happy life.

The beginning of the end for customers to decide

In the same way, do not sell to customers on the customer does not need the services or functions to increase your number. A consultative selling method allows Maybe you honest with your customers to understand what they need to address their business. This is the right approach; you may be surprised to renew it in terms of referrals and how many benefits for you.

Refuse rolling motion

You will not win every transaction, and some buyers will dislike you. That is part of the sale. Thoughtful improvement methods are essential, but it is vital to move forward quickly from rejection. Experts will refuse absolutely as evidence that you are pushing the limits. Therefore, check why your prospects are unsuccessful, seek outside opinions at the appropriate time, and move quickly and aggressively towards bigger and better deals.

Always ask to push recommended.

Successful salespeople know that the most straightforward deal usually comes from recommendations. Sales Specialist Marc Way shack built proposed requirements once a day referral Shao. Social evidence already exists, the initial promotion is straightforward, and the sales cycle is usually shorter. Once you close a successful business, always ask for a referral and quickly follow up with these potential customers.

Maintain level balance

Compared with what most professionals do in a month, salespeople experience even more significant ups and downs in a week. Sometimes, you feel invincible. A few days ago, you wanted to know if you still belonged to the sales department.

Successful sales representatives learn to control their emotions and stay in the middle. When things are going well and almost all transactions have been completed, they remind themselves not to be too arrogant. When the industry closed down, they tell me not to lose heart: if they continue to struggle, sales will pick up soon.

A breakdown
In sales, activities are usually related to results. The more emails you send, the more meetups you book. The more meetings you book, the more presentations you set up. The more displays you set, the more you complete the transaction and more.

According to this line of thinking, many salespeople every working day every day to work 10 Genial when even spend some time at the weekend.

This is not only detrimental to your physical and mental health but also no avail. Pointed out the way, some of the highest achievements of human history - such as Kobe - Bryant, LeBron - James, Cha Eris · Dickens, and Cha Eris · da Er article, both the sleep and balanced work on the priority. Something actual proof, rest can improve memory, attention, and thinking quality.

If you regularly both ends of the fuel-burning candle, then eventually exhausted. In addition, how much work was completed between 6:30 and 8:30 in the evening? During this time:

1. Have eight or more hours of sleep

Think you can sleep for five to six hours? Think again. According to the AA of Sleep Medicine, most adults need sleep every night. If reduced, you will suffer from various diseases, including:

- Easy anger
- Under power down
- Coke into account
- Symptoms of depression-like
- Divided heart
- Reducing the energy source
- Tired workers
- Manic action is not safe
- Decision not forces
- Error by plus
- Kin forget

To stay in the pro condition on the sales call, please give priority to sleep.

I believe you are selling East-West

When you genuinely believe in a product, it's easier to be passionate about it and sell it. The most effective salespeople use their products and believe in their value.

If you are "satisfied" with the products you sell, please ask customers for good recommendations. Examples of how the product can improve people's lives (big or small) will boost your motivation (and provide you with valuable social proof when meeting with potential customers!)

Identify the most powerful dynamic force.
Push factors moving the sales staff does not matter - he only needs to be motivated to. Every senior salesperson has an urgent reason to go to work every day and go all out. Maybe they want to buy a house; they must at least 110 % of the quota every month. Also promised them super competitive and always wanted to be the leader in the leaderboard. Maybe they need to prove to themselves that they can do an excellent job in sales.

Ask yourself, "I want the biggest reason for success is what it? "If you cannot answer immediately made, you need to find the motivation.

The customer success as their households to work
Potential customers, after users sign on the dotted line, the sales staff will not stop working. Instead, senior representatives often deal with customers to seek feedback and provide tactical advice.
Effective representation of life habits used to

To establish interpersonal relations department
I was one of the best salesmen know Dan - Di Er (Dan Tire) is an established human relation. Tire to his people at the link - not to surface,

LinkedIn way or "let's exchange cards" way, but with a Zhong accurate, natural, humane way, so you want to talk to him again.

As a salesman, relationships your capital. You do not need to Don - Draper (Don Draper) charm. On the contrary, the desire to help goes far beyond the character of personality.

He had earlier quasi- prepared
An effective salesperson will prepare before calling. This means they will conduct prospective customer surveys and gather all the information before large customer meetings.

The top representatives are not firm. They made plans and emergency plans. In this way, they can anticipate challenges or problems and make effective responses to avoid losing sales.

At any time, anywhere to find a potential customer household
To perform well, you can't stop being a salesperson after you leave the office. Successful sales reps are always at parties, looking for potential customers on social activities, dinners, and so on.
Of course, you must have to read the room. Should you give a five-minute speech on the importance of life insurance at the Cousin Jack Memorial? of course not. However, if you are working with a new friend Greta (Greta pay), talking about, and she referred to his being on the life insurance market, please give her some handy tips, and let her know that you'll be happy to discuss further.

Conclusion

I hope you enjoyed this book, as I enjoyed writing it. Every salesperson should read *this book*. It is a guide to hold at the bedside or on the maintenance room table—a book to fall into as needed, to scan in now and then, to enjoy in small sharp portions. It is a book for times and for the times, a book to turn to over and over again, as to a colleague, a book of pure, pure and decent leadership, an endless source of support and motivation."

www.ingramcontent.com/pod-product-compliance
Lightning Source LLC
Chambersburg PA
CBHW052325220526
45472CB00001B/276